Harvard Business Review

ON
BRINGING YOUR
WHOLE SELF TO WORK

THE HARVARD BUSINESS REVIEW PAPERBACK SERIES

The series is designed to bring today's managers and professionals the fundamental information they need to stay competitive in a fast-moving world. From the preeminent thinkers whose work has defined an entire field to the rising stars who will redefine the way we think about business, here are the leading minds and landmark ideas that have established the *Harvard Business Review* as required reading for ambitious businesspeople in organizations around the globe.

Other books in the series:

Other books in the series (continued):

Harvard Business Review on the Mind of the Leader

Harvard Business Review on Motivating People

Harvard Business Review on Negotiation and Conflict Resolution

Harvard Business Review on Nonprofits

Harvard Business Review on Organizational Learning

Harvard Business Review on Strategic Alliances

Harvard Business Review on Strategic Sales Management

Harvard Business Review on Strategies for Growth

Harvard Business Review on Supply-Chain Management

Harvard Business Review on Teams That Succeed

Harvard Business Review on the Tests of a Leader

Harvard Business Review on Top-Line Growth

Harvard Business Review on Turnarounds

Harvard Business Review on Women in Business

Harvard Business Review on Work and Life Balance

Harvard Business Review

ON

BRINGING YOUR

WHOLE SELF TO WORK

A HARVARD BUSINESS REVIEW PAPERBACK

The *Harvard Business Review* articles in this collection are available as individual reprints. Discounts apply to quantity purchases. For information and ordering, please contact Customer Service, Harvard Business School Publishing, Boston, MA 02163. Telephone: (617) 783-7500 or (800) 988-0886, 8 A.M. to 6 P.M. Eastern Time, Monday through Friday. Fax: (617) 783-7555, 24 hours a day. E-mail: custserv@hbsp.harvard.edu.

Library of Congress Cataloging-in-Publication Data
Harvard business review on bringing your whole self to work.
     p. cm. — (The Harvard business review paperback series)
    Includes index.
    ISBN-978-1-4221-2109-2
    1. Quality of work life. 2. Job satisfaction. 3. Well-being.
HD6955.H353 2008
650.1—dc22   2007037429

Contents

Harvard Business Review

ON
BRINGING YOUR
WHOLE SELF TO WORK

Overloaded Circuits

Why Smart People Underperform

EDWARD M. HALLOWELL

Executive Summary

FRENZIED EXECUTIVES WHO FIDGET through meetings, lose track of their appointments, and jab at the "door close" button on the elevator aren't crazy—just crazed. They suffer from a newly recognized neurological phenomenon that the author, a psychiatrist, calls attention deficit trait, or ADT. It isn't an illness; it's purely a response to the hyperkinetic environment in which we live. But it has become epidemic in today's organizations.

When a manager is desperately trying to deal with more input than he possibly can, the brain and body get locked into a reverberating circuit while the brain's frontal lobes lose their sophistication, as if vinegar were added to wine. The result is black-and-white thinking; perspective and shades of gray disappear. People with ADT have difficulty staying organized, setting priorities, and managing time, and they feel a constant low level of panic and guilt.

ADT can be controlled by engineering one's environment and one's emotional and physical health. Make time every few hours for a "human moment," a face-to-face exchange with a person you like. Get enough sleep, switch to a good diet, and get adequate exercise. Break down large tasks into smaller ones, and keep a section of your work space clear. Try keeping a portion of your day free of appointments and e-mail.

The author recommends that companies invest in amenities that contribute to a positive atmosphere. Leaders can also help prevent ADT by matching employees' skills to tasks. When managers assign goals that stretch people too far or ask workers to focus on what they're not good at, stress rises. ADT is a very real threat to all of us. If we don't manage it, it will manage us.

D AVID DRUMS HIS FINGERS on his desk as he scans the e-mail on his computer screen. At the same time, he's talking on the phone to an executive halfway around the world. His knee bounces up and down like a jackhammer. He intermittently bites his lip and reaches for his constant companion, the coffee cup. He's so deeply involved in multitasking that he has forgotten the appointment his Outlook calendar reminded him of 15 minutes ago.

Jane, a senior vice president, and Mike, her CEO, have adjoining offices so they can communicate quickly, yet communication never seems to happen. "Whenever I go into Mike's office, his phone lights up, my cell phone goes off, someone knocks on the door, he suddenly turns to his screen and writes an e-mail, or he tells me about a new issue he wants me to address," Jane complains. "We're working flat out just to stay afloat, and we're not getting anything important accomplished. It's driving me crazy."

David, Jane, and Mike aren't crazy, but they're certainly crazed. Their experience is becoming the norm for overworked managers who suffer—like many of your colleagues, and possibly like you—from a very real but unrecognized neurological phenomenon that I call attention deficit trait, or ADT. Caused by brain overload, ADT is now epidemic in organizations. The core symptoms are distractibility, inner frenzy, and impatience. People with ADT have difficulty staying organized, setting priorities, and managing time. These symptoms can undermine the work of an otherwise gifted executive. If David, Jane, Mike, and the millions like them understood themselves in neurological terms, they could actively manage their lives instead of reacting to problems as they happen.

As a psychiatrist who has diagnosed and treated thousands of people over the past 25 years for a medical condition called attention deficit disorder, or ADD (now known clinically as attention-deficit/hyperactivity disorder), I have observed firsthand how a rapidly growing segment of the adult population is developing this new, related condition. The number of people with ADT coming into my clinical practice has mushroomed by a factor of ten in the past decade. Unfortunately, most of the remedies for chronic overload proposed by time-management consultants and executive coaches do not address the underlying causes of ADT.

Unlike ADD, a neurological disorder that has a genetic component and can be aggravated by environmental and physical factors, ADT springs entirely from the environment. Like the traffic jam, ADT is an artifact of modern life. It is brought on by the demands on our time and attention that have exploded over the past two decades. As our minds fill with noise—feckless synaptic events signifying nothing—the brain gradually loses its capacity to attend fully and thoroughly to anything.

The symptoms of ADT come upon a person gradually. The sufferer doesn't experience a single crisis but rather a series of minor emergencies while he or she tries harder and harder to keep up. Shouldering a responsibility to "suck it up" and not complain as the workload increases, executives with ADT do whatever they can to handle a load they simply cannot manage as well as they'd like. The ADT sufferer therefore feels a constant low level of panic and guilt. Facing a tidal wave of tasks, the executive becomes increasingly hurried, curt, peremptory, and unfocused, while pretending that everything is fine.

To control ADT, we first have to recognize it. And control it we must, if we as individuals and organizational leaders are to be effective. In the following pages, I'll offer an analysis of the origins of ADT and provide some suggestions that may help you manage it.

Attention Deficit Cousins

To understand the nature and treatment of ADT, it's useful to know something of its cousin, ADD.

Usually seen as a learning disability in children, ADD also afflicts about 5% of the adult population. Researchers using MRI scans have found that people with ADD suffer a slightly diminished volume in four specific brain regions that have various functions such as modulating emotion (especially anger and frustration) and assisting in learning. One of the regions, made up of the frontal and prefrontal lobes, generates thoughts, makes decisions, sets priorities, and organizes activities. While the medications used to treat ADD don't change the anatomy of the brain, they alter brain chemistry, which in turn improves function in each of the four regions and so dramatically bolsters the performance of ADD sufferers.

ADD confers both disadvantages and advantages. The negative characteristics include a tendency to procrastinate and miss deadlines. People with ADD struggle with disorganization and tardiness; they can be forgetful and drift away mentally in the middle of a conversation or while reading. Their performance can be inconsistent: brilliant one moment and unsatisfactory the next. ADD sufferers also tend to demonstrate impatience and lose focus unless, oddly enough, they are under stress or handling multiple inputs. (This is because stress leads to the production of adrenaline, which is chemically similar to the medications we use to treat ADD.) Finally, people with ADD sometimes also self-medicate with excessive alcohol or other substances.

On the positive side, those with ADD usually possess rare talents and gifts. Those gifts often go unnoticed or undeveloped, however, because of the problems caused by the condition's negative symptoms. ADD sufferers can be remarkably creative and original. They are unusually persistent under certain circumstances and often possess an entrepreneurial flair. They display ingenuity and encourage that trait in others. They tend to improvise well under pressure. Because they have the ability to field multiple inputs simultaneously, they can be strong leaders during times of change. They also tend to rebound quickly after setbacks and bring fresh energy to the company every day.

Executives with ADD typically achieve inconsistent results. Sometimes they fail miserably because they're disorganized and make mistakes. At other times, they perform brilliantly, offering original ideas and strategies that lead to performance at the highest level.

David Neeleman, the CEO of JetBlue Airways, has ADD. School was torture; unable to focus, he hated to study and procrastinated endlessly. "I felt like I should be out doing things, moving things along, but here I was, stuck studying statistics, which I knew had no application to my life," Neeleman told me. "I knew I had to have an education, but at the first opportunity to start a business, I just blew out of college." He climbed quickly in the corporate world, making use of his strengths—original thinking, high energy, an ability to draw out the best in people—and getting help with organization and time management.

Like most people with ADD, Neeleman could sometimes offend with his blunt words, but his ideas were good enough to change the airline industry. For example, he invented the electronic ticket. "When I proposed that idea, people laughed at me, saying no one would go to the airport without a paper ticket," he says. "Now everyone does, and it has saved the industry millions of dollars." It seems fitting that someone with ADD would invent a way around having to remember to bring a paper ticket. Neeleman believes ADD is one of the keys to his success. Far from regretting having it, he celebrates it. But he understands that he must manage his ADD carefully.

Attention deficit trait is characterized by ADD's negative symptoms. Rather than being rooted in genetics, however, ADT is purely a response to the hyperkinetic environment in which we live. Indeed, modern culture all but requires many of us to develop ADT. Never in history has the human brain been asked to track so many data points. Everywhere, people rely on their cell phones, e-mail, and digital assistants in the race to gather and transmit data, plans, and ideas faster and faster. One could argue that the chief value of the modern era is speed, which the novelist Milan Kundera described as "the form of ecstasy that technology has bestowed upon modern man." Addicted to speed, we demand it even when we can't possibly go faster. James Gleick wryly noted in *Faster: The Acceleration of Just About Everything* that the "close door" button in elevators is often the one with the paint worn off. As the human brain struggles to keep up, it falters and then falls into the world of ADT.

This Is Your Brain

While brain scans cannot display anatomical differences between people with "normal" brains and people suffering from ADT, studies have shown that as the human brain is asked to process dizzying amounts of data, its ability to solve problems flexibly and creatively declines and the number of mistakes increases. To find out why, let's go on a brief neurological journey.

Blessed with the largest cortex in all of nature, owners of this trillion-celled organ today put singular pressure on the frontal and prefrontal lobes, which I'll refer to in this article as simply the frontal lobes. This region governs what is called, aptly enough, executive functioning (EF). EF guides decision making and planning; the organization and prioritization of information and ideas; time management; and various other sophisticated, uniquely human, managerial tasks. As long as our frontal lobes remain in charge, everything is fine.

Beneath the frontal lobes lie the parts of the brain devoted to survival. These deep centers govern basic functions like sleep, hunger, sexual desire, breathing, and heart rate, as well as crudely positive and negative emotions. When you are doing well and operating at peak level, the deep centers send up messages of excitement, satisfaction, and joy. They pump up your motivation, help you maintain attention, and don't interfere with working memory, the number of data points you can keep track of at once. But when you are confronted with the sixth decision after the fifth interruption in the midst of a search for the ninth missing piece of information on the day that the third deal has collapsed and the 12th impossible request has blipped unbidden across your computer screen, your brain begins to panic, reacting just as if that sixth decision were a bloodthirsty, man-eating tiger.

As a specialist in learning disabilities, I have found that the most dangerous disability is not any formally diagnosable condition like dyslexia or ADD. It is fear. Fear shifts us into survival mode and thus prevents fluid learning and nuanced understanding. Certainly, if a real tiger is about to attack you, survival is the mode you want to be in. But if you're trying to deal intelligently with a subtle task, survival mode is highly unpleasant and counterproductive.

When the frontal lobes approach capacity and we begin to fear that we can't keep up, the relationship between the higher and lower regions of the brain takes an ominous turn. Thousands of years of evolution have taught the higher brain not to ignore the lower brain's distress signals. In survival mode, the deep areas of the brain assume control and begin to direct the higher regions. As a result, the whole brain gets caught in a neurological catch-22. The deep regions interpret the messages of overload they receive from the frontal lobes in the same way they interpret everything: primitively. They furiously fire signals of fear, anxiety, impatience, irritability, anger, or panic. These alarm signals shanghai the attention of the frontal lobes, forcing them to forfeit much of their power. Because survival signals are irresistible, the frontal lobes get stuck sending messages back to the deep centers saying, "Message received. Trying to work on it but without success." These messages further perturb the deep centers, which send even more powerful messages of distress back up to the frontal lobes.

Meanwhile, in response to what's going on in the brain, the rest of the body—particularly the endocrine, respiratory, cardiovascular, musculoskeletal, and peripheral nervous systems—has shifted into crisis mode and changed its baseline physiology from peace and quiet to red alert. The brain and body are locked in a reverberating circuit while the frontal lobes lose their sophistication, as if vinegar were added to wine. In this state, EF reverts to simpleminded black-and-white thinking; perspective and shades of gray disappear. Intelligence dims. In a futile attempt to do more than is possible, the brain paradoxically reduces its ability to think clearly.

This neurological event occurs when a manager is desperately trying to deal with more input than he possibly can. In survival mode, the manager makes impulsive judgments, angrily rushing to bring closure to whatever matter is at hand. He feels compelled to get the problem under control immediately, to extinguish the perceived danger lest it destroy him. He is robbed of his flexibility, his sense of humor, his ability to deal with the unknown. He forgets the big picture and the goals and values he stands for. He loses his creativity and his ability to change plans. He desperately wants to kill the metaphorical tiger. At these moments he is prone to melting down, to throwing a tantrum, to blaming others, and to sabotaging himself. Or he may go in the opposite direction, falling into denial and total avoidance of the problems attacking him, only to be devoured. This is ADT at its worst.

Though ADT does not always reach such extreme proportions, it does wreak havoc among harried workers. Because no two brains are alike, some people deal with the condition better than others. Regardless of how well executives appear to function, however, no one has total control over his or her executive functioning.

Managing ADT

Unfortunately, top management has so far viewed the symptoms of ADT through the distorting lens of morality or character. Employees who seem unable to keep up the pace are seen as deficient or weak. Consider the case of an executive who came to see me when he was completely overloaded. I suggested he talk the situation over with his superior and ask for help. When my client did so, he was told that if he couldn't handle the work, he ought to think about resigning. Even though his performance assessments were stellar and he'd earned praise for being one of the most creative people in the organization, he was allowed to leave. Because the firm sought to preserve the myth that no straw would ever break its people's backs, it could not tolerate the manager's stating that his back was breaking. After he went out on his own, he flourished.

How can we control the rampaging effects of ADT, both in ourselves and in our organizations? While ADD often requires medication, the treatment of ADT certainly does not. ADT can be controlled only by creatively engineering one's environment and one's emotional and physical health. I have found that the following preventive measures go a long way toward helping executives control their symptoms of ADT.

PROMOTE POSITIVE EMOTIONS

The most important step in controlling ADT is not to buy a superturbocharged BlackBerry and fill it up with to-dos but rather to create an environment in which the brain can function at its best. This means building a positive, fear-free emotional atmosphere, because emotion is the on/off switch for executive functioning.

There are neurological reasons why ADT occurs less in environments where people are in physical contact and where they trust and respect one another. When you comfortably connect with a colleague, even if you are dealing with an overwhelming problem, the deep centers of the brain send messages through the pleasure center to the area that assigns resources to the frontal lobes. Even when you're under extreme stress, this sense of human connection causes executive functioning to hum.

By contrast, people who work in physical isolation are more likely to suffer from ADT, for the more isolated we are, the more stressed we become. I witnessed a dramatic example of the danger of a disconnected environment and the healing power of a connected one when I consulted for one of the world's foremost university chemistry departments. In the department's formerly hard-driven culture, ADT was rampant, exacerbated by an ethic that forbade anyone to ask for help or even state that anything was wrong. People did not trust one another; they worked on projects alone, which led to more mistrust. Most people were in emotional pain, but implicit in the department's culture was the notion that great pain led to great gain.

In the late 1990s, one of the department's most gifted graduate students killed himself. His suicide note explicitly blamed the university for pushing him past his limit. The department's culture was literally lethal.

Instead of trying to sweep the tragedy under the rug, the chair of the department and his successor acted boldly and creatively. They immediately changed the structure of the supervisory system so that each graduate student and postdoc was assigned three supervisors, rather than a single one with a death grip on the trainee's career. The department set up informal biweekly buffets that allowed people to connect. (Even the most reclusive chemist came out of hiding for food, one of life's great connectors.) The department heads went as far as changing the architecture of the department's main building, taking down walls and adding common areas and an espresso bar complete with a grand piano. They provided lectures and written information to all students about the danger signs of mental wear and tear and offered confidential procedures for students who needed help. These steps, along with regular meetings that included senior faculty and university administrators, led to a more humane, productive culture in which the students and faculty felt fully engaged. The department's performance remained first-rate, and creative research blossomed.

The bottom line is this: Fostering connections and reducing fear promote brainpower. When you make time at least every four to six hours for a "human moment," a face-to-face exchange with a person you like, you are giving your brain what it needs.

TAKE PHYSICAL CARE OF YOUR BRAIN

Sleep, a good diet, and exercise are critical for staving off ADT. Though this sounds like a no-brainer, too many of us abuse our brains by neglecting obvious principles of care.

You may try to cope with ADT by sleeping less, in the vain hope that you can get more done. This is the opposite of what you need to do, for ADT sets in when you don't get enough sleep. There is ample documentation to suggest that sleep deprivation engenders a host of problems, from impaired decision making and reduced creativity to reckless behavior and paranoia. We vary in how much sleep we require; a good rule of thumb is that you're getting enough sleep if you can wake up without an alarm clock.

Diet also plays a crucial role in brain health. Many hardworking people habitually inhale carbohydrates, which cause blood glucose levels to yo-yo. This leads to a vicious cycle: Rapid fluctuations in insulin levels further increase the craving for carbohydrates. The brain, which relies on glucose for energy, is left either glutted or gasping, neither of which makes for optimal cognitive functioning.

The brain does much better if the blood glucose level can be held relatively stable. To do this, avoid simple carbohydrates containing sugar and white flour (pastries, white bread, and pasta, for example). Rely on the complex carbohydrates found in fruits, whole grains, and vegetables. Protein is important: Instead of starting your

day with coffee and a Danish, try tea and an egg or a
piece of smoked salmon on wheat toast. Take a multivitamin every day as well as supplementary omega-3 fatty
acids, an excellent source of which is fish oil. The omega-
3s and the E and B complex contained in multivitamins
promote healthy brain function and may even stave off
Alzheimer's disease and inflammatory ills (which can be
the starting point for major killers like heart disease,
stroke, diabetes, and cancer). Moderate your intake of
alcohol, too, because too much kills brain cells and accelerates the development of memory loss and even demen-
tia. As you change your diet to promote optimal brain
function and good general health, your body will also
shed excess pounds.

If you think you can't afford the time to exercise,
think again. Sitting at a desk for hours on end decreases
mental acuity, not only because of reduced blood flow to
the brain but for other biochemical reasons as well. Physical exercise induces the body to produce an array of
chemicals that the brain loves, including endorphins,
serotonin, dopamine, epinephrine, and norepinephrine,
as well as two recently discovered compounds, brain-
derived neurotrophic factor (BDNF) and nerve growth
factor (NGF). Both BDNF and NGF promote cell health
and development in the brain, stave off the ravages of
aging and stress, and keep the brain in tip-top condition.
Nothing stimulates the production of BDNF and NGF as
robustly as physical exercise, which explains why those
who exercise regularly talk about the letdown and slug-
gishness they experience if they miss their exercise for a
few days. You will more than compensate for the time
you invest on the treadmill with improved productivity
and efficiency. To fend off the symptoms of ADT while
you're at work, get up from your desk and go up and

down a flight of stairs a few times or walk briskly down a
hallway. These quick, simple efforts will push your
brain's reset button.

ORGANIZE FOR ADT

It's important to develop tactics for getting organized,
but not in the sense of empty New Year's resolutions.
Rather, your goal is to order your work in a way that suits
you, so that disorganization does not keep you from
reaching your goals.

First, devise strategies to help your frontal lobes stay
in control. These might include breaking down large
tasks into smaller ones and keeping a section of your
work space or desk clear at all times. (You do not need to
have a neat office, just a neat section of your office.) Similarly, you might try keeping a portion of your day free of
appointments, e-mail, and other distractions so that you
have time to think and plan. Because e-mail is a wonderful way to procrastinate and set yourself up for ADT
at the same time, you might consider holding specific
"e-mail hours," since it isn't necessary to reply to every
e-mail right away.

When you start your day, don't allow yourself to get
sucked into vortices of e-mail or voice mail or into
attending to minor tasks that eat up your time but don't
pack a punch. Attend to a critical task instead. Before
you leave for the day, make a list of no more than five priority items that will require your attention tomorrow.
Short lists force you to prioritize and complete your
tasks. Additionally, keep torrents of documents at bay.
One of my patients, an executive with ADD, uses the
OHIO rule: Only handle it once. If he touches a document, he acts on it, files it, or throws it away. "I don't put

it in a pile," he says. "Piles are like weeds. If you let them grow, they take over everything."

Pay attention to the times of day when you feel that you perform at your best; do your most important work then and save the rote work for other times. Set up your office in a way that helps mental functioning. If you focus better with music, have music (if need be, use earphones). If you think best on your feet, work standing up or walk around frequently. If doodling or drumming your fingers helps, figure out a way to do so without bothering anyone, or get a fidget toy to bring to meetings. These small strategies sound mundane, but they address the ADT devil that resides in distracting details.

PROTECT YOUR FRONTAL LOBES

To stay out of survival mode and keep your lower brain from usurping control, slow down. Take the time you need to comprehend what is going on, to listen, to ask questions, and to digest what's been said so that you don't get confused and send your brain into panic. Empower an assistant to ride herd on you; insist that he or she tell you to stop e-mailing, get off the telephone, or leave the office.

If you do begin to feel overwhelmed, try the following mind-clearing tricks. Do an easy rote task, such as resetting the calendar on your watch or writing a memo on a neutral topic. If you feel anxious about beginning a project, pull out a sheet of paper or fire up your word processor and write a paragraph about something unrelated to the project (a description of your house, your car, your shoes—anything you know well). You can also tackle the easiest part of the task; for example, write just the title of a memo about it. Open a dictionary and read a few definitions, or spend five minutes doing a crossword puzzle. Each of these little tasks quiets your lower brain by tricking it into shutting off alarmist messages and puts your frontal lobes back in full control.

Finally, be ready for the next attack of ADT by posting the "Control Your ADT" insert (at the end of this article) near your desk where you can see it. Knowing that you are prepared diminishes the likelihood of an attack, because you're not susceptible to panic.

What Leaders Can Do

All too often, companies induce and exacerbate ADT in their employees by demanding fast thinking rather than deep thinking. Firms also ask employees to work on multiple overlapping projects and initiatives, resulting in second-rate thinking. Worse, companies that ask their employees to do too much at once tend to reward those who say yes to overload while punishing those who choose to focus and say no.

Moreover, organizations make the mistake of forcing their employees to do more and more with less and less by eliminating support staff. Such companies end up losing money in the long run, for the more time a manager has to spend being his own administrative assistant and the less he is able to delegate, the less effective he will be in doing the important work of moving the organization forward. Additionally, firms that ignore the symptoms of ADT in their employees suffer its ill effects: Employees underachieve, create clutter, cut corners, make careless mistakes, and squander their brain-power. As demands continue to increase, a toxic, high-pressure environment leads to high rates of employee illness and turnover.

To counteract ADT and harness employee brain-power, firms should invest in amenities that contribute to a positive atmosphere. One company that has done an excellent job in this regard is SAS Institute, a major software company in North Carolina. The company famously offers its employees a long list of perks: a 36,000-square-foot, on-site gym; a seven-hour workday that ends at 5 PM; the largest on-site day care facility in North Carolina; a cafeteria that provides baby seats and high chairs so parents can eat lunch with their children; unlimited sick days; and much more. The atmosphere at SAS is warm, connected, and relaxed. The effect on the bottom line is profoundly positive; turnover is never higher than 5%. The company saves the millions other software companies spend on recruiting, training, and severance (estimated to be at least 1.5 times salary in the software industry). Employees return the favors with high productivity. The forces of ADT that shred other organizations never gain momentum at SAS.

Leaders can also help prevent ADT by matching employees' skills to tasks. When managers assign goals that stretch people too far or ask workers to focus on what they're not good at rather than what they do well, stress rises. By contrast, managers who understand the dangers of ADT can find ways of keeping themselves and their organizations on track. JetBlue's David Neeleman, for example, has shamelessly and publicly identified what he is not good at and found ways to deal with his shortcomings, either by delegating or by empowering his assistant to direct him. Neeleman also models this behavior for everyone else in the organization. His openness about the challenges of his ADD gives others permission to speak about their own attention deficit difficulties and to garner the support they need. He also encourages his managers to match people with tasks that fit their cognitive and emotional styles, knowing that no one style is best. Neeleman believes that helping people work to their strengths is not just a mark of sophisticated management; it's also an excellent way to boost worker productivity and morale.

Aᴅᴛ ɪs ᴀ ᴠᴇʀʏ ʀᴇᴀʟ ᴛʜʀᴇᴀᴛ to all of us. If we do not manage it, it manages us. But an understanding of ADT and its ravages allows us to apply practical methods to improve our work and our lives. In the end, the most critical step an enlightened leader can take to address the problem of ADT is to name it. Bringing ADT out of the closet and describing its symptoms removes the stigma and eliminates the moral condemnation companies have for so long mistakenly leveled at overburdened employees. By giving people permission to ask for help and remaining vigilant for signs of stress, organizations will go a long way toward fostering more productive, well-balanced, and intelligent work environments.

Control Your ADT

In General

- Get adequate sleep.
- Watch what you eat. Avoid simple, sugary carbohydrates, moderate your intake of alcohol, add protein, stick to complex carbohydrates (vegetables, whole grains, fruit).
- Exercise at least 30 minutes at least every other day.
- Take a daily multivitamin and an omega-3 fatty acid supplement.

At Work

- Do all you can to create a trusting, connected work environment.

- Have a friendly, face-to-face talk with a person you like every four to six hours.

- Break large tasks into smaller ones.

- Keep a section of your work space or desk clear at all times.

- Each day, reserve some "think time" that's free from appointments, e-mail, and phone calls.

- Set aside e-mail until you've completed at least one or two more important tasks.

- Before you leave work each day, create a short list of three to five items you will attend to the next day.

- Try to act on, file, or toss every document you touch.

- Don't let papers accumulate.

- Pay attention to the times of day when you feel that you are at your best; do your most important work then, and save the rote work for other times.

- Do whatever you need to do to work in a more focused way: Add background music, walk around, and so on.

- Ask a colleague or an assistant to help you stop talking on the telephone, e-mailing, or working too late.

When You Feel Overwhelmed

- Slow down.

- Do an easy rote task: Reset your watch, write a note about a neutral topic (such as a description of your house), read a few dictionary definitions, do a short crossword puzzle.

- Move around: Go up and down a flight of stairs or walk briskly.

- Ask for help, delegate a task, or brainstorm with a colleague. In short, do not worry alone.

Originally published in January 2005
Reprint R0501E

The Human Moment at Work

EDWARD M. HALLOWELL

Executive Summary

IN THE LAST DECADE OR SO, technological changes—mainly voice mail and e-mail—have made a lot of face-to-face interaction unnecessary. Face-to-face contact has also fallen victim to "virtuality"—many people work at home or are otherwise off-site. Indeed, most people today can't imagine life without such technology and the freedom it grants.

But Edward Hallowell, a noted psychiatrist who has been treating patients with anxiety disorders—many of them business executives—for more than 20 years, warns that we are in danger of losing what he calls the *human moment:* an authentic psychological encounter that can happen only when two people share the same physical space. And, he believes, we may be about to discover the destructive power of its absence.

The author relates stories of businesspeople who have dealt firsthand with the misunderstandings caused by an overreliance on technology. An e-mail message is misconstrued. Someone forwards a voice-mail message to the wrong people. A person takes offense because he was not included on a certain circulation list. Was it an accident? Often the consequences of such misunderstandings, taken individually, are minor. Over time, however, they take a larger toll—both on individuals and on the organizations they work for.

The problem, however, is not insoluble. The author cites examples of people who have worked successfully to restore face-to-face contact in their organizations. The bottom line is that the strategic use of the human moment adds color to our lives and helps us build confidence and trust at work. We ignore it at our peril.

THE CHIEF FINANCIAL OFFICER of an international consulting firm holds a cell phone to his ear while waiting for the shuttle from New York to Boston. He listens to the messages that have piled up since he phoned in three hours earlier. After he flips the phone closed, he sits down to wait for his plane and starts to brood. A valued employee has asked for a transfer to another division. Questions begin to ricochet through his mind: What if the employee complains that the CFO is a lousy boss? What if the employee plans to take his team with him in the move? What if, what if . . . ? The CFO becomes lost in a frightening tangle of improbable outcomes, a thicket that will ensnarl his mind the entire flight back to Boston. The minute he gets home he will dash off an e-mail to the employee and eagerly await a reply—which, when it comes the next day, will likely upset him further by its ambiguity. More brooding will ensue, making it difficult for him to focus on his work.

At an electronics company, a talented brand manager is growing increasingly alienated. The problem started when his division head didn't return a phone call for several days. She said she never got the message. Then the brand manager noticed that he hadn't been invited to an important meeting with a new advertising agency. What's wrong with my performance? he wonders. The man wants to raise the question with the division manager, but the opportunity never seems to arise. All their communication is by memo, e-mail, or voice mail, which they exchange often. But they almost never meet. For one thing, their offices are 50 miles apart, and for another, both of them are frequently on the road. During the rare moments when they do see each other in person—on the run in a corridor or in the parking lot at corporate headquarters—it is usually inappropriate or impossible to discuss complex matters. And so the issues between them smolder.

In both scenarios, the executives' anxiety has a simple antidote: a face-to-face conversation. Both men are driving themselves crazy for no reason. But to learn that, they need to reconnect with their unwitting partners in (emotional) crime—and they need to do it in person. They need to experience what I call *the human moment:* an authentic psychological encounter that can happen only when two people share the same physical space. I have given the human moment a name because I believe that it has started to disappear from modern life—and I sense that we all may be about to discover the destructive power of its absence.

The human moment has two prerequisites: people's physical presence and their emotional and intellectual attention. That's it. Physical presence alone isn't enough; you can ride shoulder-to-shoulder with someone for six hours in an airplane and not have a human moment the entire ride. And attention alone isn't enough either. You can pay attention to someone over the telephone, for instance, but somehow phone conversations lack the power of true human moments.

Human moments require energy. Often, that's what makes them easy to avoid. The human moment may be seen as yet another tax on our overextended lives. But a human moment doesn't have to be emotionally draining or personally revealing. In fact, the human moment can be brisk, businesslike, and brief. A five-minute conversation can be a perfectly meaningful human moment. To make the human moment work, you have to set aside what you're doing, put down the memo you were reading, disengage from your laptop, abandon your daydream, and focus on the person you're with. Usually when you do that, the other person will feel the energy and respond in kind. Together, you quickly create a force field of exceptional power.

The positive effects of a human moment can last long after the people involved have said goodbye and walked away. People begin to think in new and creative ways; mental activity is stimulated. But like exercise, which also has enduring effects, the benefits of a human moment do not last indefinitely. A ten-mile run on Monday is wonderful—but only if you also swim on Wednesday and play tennis on Saturday. In other words, you must engage in human moments on a regular basis for them to have a meaningful impact on your life. For most people, that's not a tall order.

I am concerned, however, that human moments are disappearing and that this trend will be accompanied by worrisome and widespread consequences. I say this not as an executive but as a psychiatrist who has been treating patients with anxiety disorders for 20 years. Because of where I practice and the nature of my expertise, many of my patients are senior business executives who—to the outside world—are pictures of success. But I can tell you without a doubt that virtually everyone I see is experiencing some deficiency of human contact. Indeed, I am increasingly sought out because people feel lonely, isolated, or confused at work. The treatment I provide invariably involves replenishing the human moments in their lives.

The Disappearing Human Moment

Human beings are remarkably resilient. They can deal with almost anything as long as they do not become too isolated. But my patients, as well as my acquaintances in the business world, tell me that as the tide of electronic hyperconnection rises, the landscape of work is in some ways changing for the worse. As Ray, a senior systems manager in a large investment company, told me: "I don't talk to people as much as I used to. And sometimes the results are very damaging."

Ray wasn't complaining—overall, he likes his job quite a bit—but he was concerned. "I've found you can stumble into giant misunderstandings with e-mail. People's feelings can get hurt and wrong information can get picked up."

As an example, he told the following story. "A guy sent me an e-mail that said, 'We were not able to access the following application, and we need to know why,' and he cc'd his supervisor, solely to show the supervisor that he was doing something about the problem. What bugged me was that line, 'and we need to know why.' If he had spoken to me face-to-face we could have solved the problem, but no, I get this e-mail with its peremptory tone, and he's cc'd it. My immediate response was, back at you. So I write an officious sounding e-mail, with a cc to a bunch of other people, including his supervisor, explaining that I had submitted a change management ticket, and if he had gone to the meeting where that was discussed he would have known about it and wouldn't have even tried to access that application. I became that guy's adversary instead of solving the problem. But I felt goaded into it."

Ray's story illustrates how letting the human moment fall to the wayside leads to dysfunction in organizations. When human moments are few and far between, over-sensitivity, self-doubt, and even boorishness and abrasive curtness can be observed in the best of people. Productive employees will begin to feel lousy and that, in turn, will lead them to underperform or to think of looking elsewhere for work. The irony is that this kind of alienation in the workplace derives not from lack of communication but from a surplus of the wrong kind. The remedy is not to get rid of electronics but to restore the human moment where it is needed.

The absence of the human moment—on an organizational scale—can wreak havoc. Coworkers slowly but surely lose their sense of cohesiveness. It starts with one person, but distrust, disrespect, and dissatisfaction on the job are like contagions. Soon enough there are five or ten people like Ray and his e-mail partner, and then more. Eventually, such people make up the majority. An organization's culture turns unfriendly and unforgiving. Good people leave. Those who remain are unhappy. Mental health concerns aside, such conditions are not good for business. Indeed, they can be downright corrosive.

To be sure, people have felt lonely or isolated at work in the past. Henry Ford's early factories were no love-ins. Nevertheless, from the 1950s onward, executives and middle managers came to expect that they would talk with one another in the office—for business or personal reasons—and would even play together at the end of the day. And when it came time to connect with distant clients or suppliers or colleagues, people got on planes. Meetings happened in person. Yes, they were time consuming and costly. But they fostered trust. Not incidentally, people had more fun.

But in the last ten years or so, technological changes have made a lot of face-to-face interaction unnecessary. I'm talking about voice mail and e-mail mainly—modes of communication that are one-way and electronic. Face-to-face interaction has also fallen victim to "virtuality"— many people work at home or are otherwise off-site. I will certainly not try to make a case that these changes are bad. And indeed, no one planned on reducing face-to-face meetings; this is simply happening naturally, with the inevitability of water flowing downhill. We have the technology, so we are using it.

For the most part, it makes our lives much better. I enjoy the efficiency and freedom that voice mail and e-mail give me. I communicate with people when I want to, from any location. While I'm traveling, I keep up with my messages from patients and the office through voice mail, and I log on from hotel rooms to collect my e-mail every day. Like most people, I don't know how I ever managed without these tools.

But problems that develop when the human moment is lost cannot be ignored. People need human contact in order to survive. They need it to maintain their mental acuity and their emotional well-being. I make this assertion having listened to and counseled thousands of patients whose jobs have been sapped of human moments. And I make it based on strong evidence from the field of brain science. (See "The Brain Chemistry of the Human Moment" at the end of this article.)

Toxic Worry

What happens to the psychology of the mind when the human moment vanishes—or at least fades—from our lives? In the worst case, paranoia fills the vacuum. In my practice, that has been rare. More often, the human moment is replaced by worry. That's because electronic communications remove many of the cues that typically mitigate worry. Those cues—body language, tone of voice, and facial expression—are especially important among sophisticated people who are prone to using subtle language, irony, and wit.

Not all worry is bad, of course. Some of my patients tell me that in business, worry can be a great tool. It is an inner voice telling you that trouble—a new competitor or a new technology that will shake up your industry—is on the way. "Good worry" leads to constructive planning and corrective action; it is essential to success in any endeavor.

"Toxic worry" is another matter entirely. It is anxiety that has no basis in reality. It immobilizes the sufferer and leads to indecision or destructive action. It's like being in the dark, and we all feel paranoid in the dark. Try an experiment. Go into a room at night and turn off the lights. Your whole body will respond. Even if you know the room well, you will probably feel the hairs on the back of your neck rise up a little as you wonder who might be lurking in the corner. The human moment is like light in an otherwise dark room: it illuminates dark corners and dispels suspicions and fears. Without it, toxic worry grows.

Toxic worry is among the most debilitating consequences of vanishing human moments, but much more common are the little misunderstandings. An e-mail message is misconstrued. A voice-mail message gets forwarded to the wrong people. Someone takes offense because he is not included on a certain circulation list. Was it an accident? Such problems can be tolerated by most individuals from time to time—as I've said, people are resilient. But as the number of human moments decreases, the number of little misunderstandings is likely to increase. They compound one another until there is nothing little about them anymore. People begin to wonder if they can trust their organizations and, just as often, they begin to question their own motives, performance, and self-worth.

Consider Harry, a senior partner at a Boston law firm. Harry was representing a bank in a complicated real estate deal with the developer of a commercial property. Many of the details of the agreement were being worked out via e-mail between Harry and the developer's counsel. At a key juncture, when a technical point about interest rates came up, the developer's counsel e-mailed Harry, "Of course your client won't grasp this, because he won't understand what we're talking about." When Harry's client read this message, which was mixed in with other documents, he became furious and nearly canceled the deal. Trying to patch things up, Harry met with the developer's lawyer, who was stunned to hear how his message had been misconstrued. "I was trying to be ironic!" the lawyer gasped in horror. "Your client is an expert in the field—saying he didn't know what we were talking about was just my way of being funny. I can't believe what a misunderstanding this is!"

When he came to me, Harry was second-guessing himself, asking me if he had some unconscious wish to fail because he had allowed the message to be seen by his client. But the real problem was in the mode of communication, not in Harry's unconscious.

Harry's deal was saved, but sometimes the misunderstandings wrought by the absence of the human moment do permanent damage. I recently treated a man—let's call him Charles—who came to see me because he was waking up in the middle of the night. He was worried about the company he had just sold for $20 million.

"What's wrong?" I asked him.

"I had intended to stay on with the company for at least a couple of years, but I'm worried it's going to be impossible. I can't deal with the COO. He's in Texas, where the headquarters are, and I'm in Massachusetts, and he keeps sending me e-mails with lists of things he wants me to do. This may sound petty, but the way he phrases them just makes me crazy. When I sold the company I knew my role would change, but this is totally degrading."

"Can you give me an example?" I asked.

"Sure. I turned on my computer Monday and got an e-mail that simply said, 'Last communication unacceptable. Redo.' I replied, asking for specifics. He e-mailed me back, 'I don't have time to explain. Can't you figure it out?' Suddenly I'm feeling like a third-grader. But I tried to rise above it. The next day he e-mailed me, 'Your peo-

ple up there have to do longer weekend hours.' Then I
started to lose sleep."

"Is this their way of getting rid of you?" I asked.

"It looks like it, but the fact is that they need me. They
know that. But I can't deal with this."

"Can you talk to the COO?" I asked.

"He's evasive. When we meet, he's polite but vague.
He does all his damage through e-mail."

Although Charles was determined to make the transi-
tion and stay with the new company, his resolve broke
down as he felt increasingly at odds with headquarters,
particularly the COO. And he started to brood about the
direction and purpose of the company, issues he had felt
confident about when he made the deal. "I've become a
worrier instead of a problem solver," Charles told me. "I
never used to be this way."

When Charles submitted his letter of resignation, he
was deluged with evidence that the company did indeed
want him to stay. He received dozens of e-mail messages
and phone calls from people pleading with him to recon-
sider. But by then the damage had been done. Charles's
heart was not in it. He was getting interested in new
ideas for other businesses, and venture capitalists had
approached him the minute he leaked word of his dissatisfaction. The company's attempts to keep him proved to
be too little, too late.

When we discussed his resignation, Charles told me
how easy it would have been for the new company to
have kept him, if only he had been treated with even
minimal respect by the COO. "My problems really came
down to those e-mail interactions," he said.

It sounded as if the COO couldn't handle his competitive feelings, but instead of dealing with Charles face-to-
face, he took him on in e-mail. He used that approach as

a weapon for his negative and angry emotions. In person, he would have had to submit to social convention. His dark feelings would have been forced into the light.

The human moment, then, is a regulator: when you take it away, people's primitive instincts can get the better of them. Just as in the anonymity of an automobile, where stable people can behave like crazed maniacs, so too on a keyboard: courteous people can become rude and abrupt.

Less dramatic but more common are the instances when people come to see me because they feel worn out by all the nonhuman interactions that fill their days. "I feel like I'm going brain-dead," said Lynn, an executive at a health care company. She consulted me because she actually thought she was losing her memory. In meetings, words were not coming to her as quickly, and decisions that she once made in a snap were now taking her hours or days. Lynn had long prided herself on her sharp mind. Now she felt as if her head were swallowed by fog. But she was still wise enough to realize that her problems might be connected to the changing texture of her work. "I do 30% to 40% of my work by leaving voice-mail messages, playing phone tag, or sending e-mail," she said. "It used to be just 10%. I see and talk to people less and less and less."

A few simple tests conducted in my office revealed that Lynn's brain itself was in fine shape. However, she was right. Her work habits were diminishing her brain's performance. Your psyche, just like your muscles, actually needs rest and variation to perform at its peak. Lynn acted as if she had run a marathon through the desert. No wonder her body ached and her mind was numb. Staying on-screen, on-line, or on the telephone for extended periods—just like any other long and monotonous activity—wears you out. The brain becomes starved for fuel: rest and human contact. That is why punishments like exile and solitary confinement are so painful. All the coffee in the world can't make up for the brain-dead state that many people in jobs like Lynn's feel at about 3 o'clock in the afternoon.

The antidote to Lynn's condition was straightforward. She needed some diversity in her work life. I suggested that she refresh her mind with a bit of exercise or, even better, that she regularly seek out conversations with real, live human beings. She did so and today reports that both her work and her brain's performance are much improved. But I am concerned about all the executives out there who have not sought help as Lynn did. Although most executives attend enough meetings and social functions to prevent them from becoming zombies, the anonymity and monotony of technology can—and will—decrease their brain stamina. And for that, both individuals and organizations will pay a price.

High Tech, High Touch

A patient of mine who was a CEO once told me, "High tech requires high touch." When I asked him what he meant, he explained to me that his company had run into a problem. Every time it made another part of its operations virtual—moving salespeople entirely into the field, for instance—the company's culture suffered. So he had developed a policy that required all "virtual" employees to come into the office at least once a month for unstructured face time.

"It's like what happened when banks introduced ATMs," the CEO said. "Once people didn't know Alice behind the counter anymore or any of the lending agents behind those glass walls, the whole loan process got tougher for both the banks and the customers. There was no familiarity, no trust."

"I love ATMs," I replied.

"So do I. So does everyone," said the CEO. "But the banks have been scrambling for years now to get their customers into a relationship again. You see, for business to do well, you can't have high tech without high touch. They have to work together."

The CEO was right. But combining high tech and high touch is easier said than done, according to my patients. Technology always seems to take precedence. Recently, however, I encountered two examples of human and "virtual" moments working in tandem and reinforcing each other to great effect.

Jack is a major real-estate developer based in Boston. In the last decade, his offices and interests have become worldwide. He runs his operation from a suite of offices located on the ground floor of a Back Bay brownstone that he calls the "bat cave." A former football player at Yale, Jack considers teamwork the key to his company's success. When I asked him how he dealt with the recent growth of his company, its increasing diversification, the expanding numbers of people working for him, his reply was: "Thursday pizza."

"About ten years ago, I realized I wasn't seeing people as often as before," Jack explained. "I was running around and so was everybody else. We never got a chance to sit down and talk." Jack worried about the impact of this disconnectedness on his business, in which sharing information is critical, so he started a Thursday ritual: a free pizza lunch in the office. "I know this is not an advanced management technique, but it does the job," Jack said. "On Thursdays, we sit around the big table in my office and we talk. There is no agenda. The group averages about 15 people and changes members every week, but there is a core of 5 or 6 who provide continuity. They meet even when I'm not there. We all look forward to it not as a business meeting but as an opportunity for informal talk. People catch up with each other, they brainstorm, they bring up stuff that doesn't get discussed elsewhere, and it works." According to Jack, the pizza lunches are largely responsible for his organization's high morale and competitive strength.

Jack's pizza lunch is a simple way of maintaining the human moment at work. Sometimes, however, reinstating the human moment can be more complex. Consider the case of David, who runs a consulting firm that advises independent furniture stores. About a decade ago, he found that many of his clients were becoming increasingly isolated after an industry consolidation left only one or two independents in each city. Sales representatives from the major manufacturers wouldn't service them in person anymore. They were asked to order over the phone or through the Internet. "You used to learn what was going on in the marketplace from the sales reps who stopped by your store. And a lot of those relationships were very close," David explained. "With the sales reps gone, the independents felt completely cut off."

In response to this problem, David decided to start what he called "performance groups"—groups of independent retailers from different parts of the country who would get together three times a year to talk business and offer one another support. When he presented this idea to his colleagues at the consulting firm, they hesitated. They worried that the project might fail, given the notoriously guarded, private nature of independent furniture retailers.

But the need for the human moment proved strong. Today, six groups of independent furniture dealers exist, with ten people in each. They meet in two-day sessions with retailers in noncompeting cities. "We've had people in our groups who say that their fathers would roll over in their graves if they knew they were sharing the financials of their company with other retailers," David told me. "But sharing those financials creates trust and a bond. These people share their best ideas, they benchmark performance, and they give one another the support they need."

The sessions can be very emotional, according to David. "We've had guys break down in tears when people in the group have looked at them and said, 'Fire your son.' But the groups put them in touch with people who know the business and can help work things out." They have provided a human moment.

It's important to note that the groups' face-to-face meetings are augmented by electronic communication. The performance groups use e-mail and other electronic means to support and expand what they do in the meetings. But David believes the in-person meetings are indispensable. "I think a sense of caring develops when you're dealing with somebody face-to-face. Over the Internet you tend to be very precise with questions and answers, and you can't register people's emotions. People don't open up over the Internet like they do in person. When you're chatting with somebody, you can see by his facial expression that you've hit on a very sensitive subject. It may be a signal to avoid that subject or it may be a signal to go further. You can't tell that over the computer." But David feels strongly that the Internet is valuable. In fact, he is currently creating a chat room for each performance group. Using a code to enter, members will be able to "talk" between meetings, thereby sustaining, and even building on, the important relationships forged face-to-face.

The performance groups in the retail furniture business seem to me a brilliant example of using the human moment judiciously—even strategically. Obviously, we don't want to turn back the clock and dispense with the tremendous efficiencies afforded us by electronic communications, but we do need to learn how to deal with the hidden problems they can create.

Indeed, the strategic use of the human moment can help reduce the confusion and ambiguity of electronic communications, develop confidence and trust as only in-person meetings can, and reduce the toxic worry, mental fatigue, and disconnection associated with the excessive use of electronics.

Technology has created a magnificent new world, bursting with opportunity. It has opened up a global, knowledge-based economy and unchained people from their desks. We are all in its debt—and we're never going back. But we cannot move forward successfully without preserving the human moment. The price we pay for not doing that is too high, for individuals and organizations alike. The human moment provides the zest and color in the painting of our daily lives; it restores us, strengthens us, and makes us whole. Luckily, as long as we arrange our lives properly, the human moment should be easy enough to preserve. All we have to do is take heed—and make it happen.

The Brain Chemistry of the Human Moment

THE ANECDOTAL EVIDENCE COMPILED during my work as a psychiatrist and researcher over 20 years strongly suggests that a deficit of the human moment damages a person's emotional health. That finding is also supported by an ever growing body of scientific research.

Working as long ago as the 1940s, the French psychoanalyst Rene Spitz showed that infants who were not held, stroked, and cuddled—even if they had parents who fed and clothed them—suffered from retarded neurological development. In 1951, researchers at McGill University found that a lack of normal contact with the outside world played havoc with adults' sense of reality. In the study, 14 men and women were placed in sensory deprivation tanks; within hours, all of them reported an altered sense of reality, insomnia—even hallucinations.

More recent studies have examined less extreme situations with equally compelling results. Between 1965 and 1974, two epidemiologists studied the lifestyles and health of 4,725 residents of Alameda County, California. They found that death rates were three times as high for socially isolated people as for those with strong connections to others. A similar study of Seattle residents, published in 1997, found that married people with a strong social network had lower health care costs and fewer primary care visits than those who were more isolated. Still other studies have shown that supportive social relationships boost immune-system responsiveness and prolong life after heart attacks.

Consider also the decade-long MacArthur Foundation study on aging in the United States, which was recently completed by a team of eminent scientists from around the country. It showed that the top two predictors of well-being as people age are frequency of visits with friends and frequency of attendance at meetings of organizations. The study also discovered that, although those who have religious beliefs on average live longer than those who don't, people who actually *attend* religious services do better than those who believe but do not go to services.

Most recently, researchers from Carnegie Mellon University examined how people were affected by spending time on-line. Contrary to their expectations, they found higher levels of depression and loneliness in people who spend even a few hours per week connected to the Internet. Again, this suggests that the electronic world, while useful in many respects, is not an adequate substitute for the world of human contact.

What exactly is the chemistry at work in these studies of brain function? Scientists don't know the whole story yet, but they do know that positive human-to-human contact reduces the blood levels of the stress hormones epinephrine, norepinephrine, and cortisol.

Nature also equips us with hormones that promote trust and bonding: oxytocin and vasopressin. Most abundant in nursing mothers, these hormones are always present to some degree in all of us, but they rise when we feel empathy for another person—in particular when we are meeting with someone face-to-face. It has been shown that these bonding hormones are at suppressed levels when people are physically separate, which is one of the reasons that it is easier to deal harshly with someone via e-mail than in person. Furthermore, scientists hypothesize that in-person contact stimulates two important neurotransmitters: dopamine, which enhances attention and pleasure, and serotonin, which reduces fear and worry.

Science, in other words, tells the same story as my patients. The human moment is neglected at the brain's peril.

Originally published in January–February 1999
Reprint 99104

The Making of a Corporate Athlete

JIM LOEHR AND TONY SCHWARTZ

Executive Summary

MANAGEMENT THEORISTS HAVE LONG SOUGHT to identify precisely what makes some people flourish under pressure and others fold. But they have come up with only partial answers: rich material rewards, the right culture, management by objectives. The problem with most approaches is that they deal with people only from the neck up, connecting high performance primarily with cognitive capacity. Authors Loehr and Schwartz argue that a successful approach to sustained high performance must consider the person as a whole. Executives are, in effect, "corporate athletes." If they are to perform at high levels over the long haul, they must train in the systematic, multilevel way that athletes do.

Rooted in two decades of work with world-class athletes, the integrated theory of performance management addresses the body, the emotions, the mind, and the spirit through a model the authors call the performance pyramid. At its foundation is physical well-being. Above that rest emotional health, then mental acuity, and, finally, a spiritual purpose. Each level profoundly influences the others, and all must be addressed together to avoid compromising performance. Rigorous exercise, for instance, can produce a sense of emotional well-being, clearing the way for peak mental performance. Rituals that promote oscillation—the rhythmic expenditure and recovery of energy—link the levels of the pyramid and lead to the ideal performance state.

The authors offer case studies of executives who have used the model to increase professional performance and improve the quality of their lives. In a corporate environment that is changing at warp speed, performing consistently at high levels is more necessary than ever. Companies can't afford to address employees' cognitive capacities while ignoring their physical, emotional, and spiritual well-being.

IF THERE IS ONE QUALITY that executives seek for themselves and their employees, it is sustained high performance in the face of ever-increasing pressure and rapid change. But the source of such performance is as elusive as the fountain of youth. Management theorists have long sought to identify precisely what makes some people flourish under pressure and others fold. We maintain that they have come up with only partial answers: rich material rewards, the right culture, management by objectives.

The problem with most approaches, we believe, is that they deal with people only from the neck up, connecting high performance primarily with cognitive capacity. In recent years there has been a growing focus on the relationship between emotional intelligence and high performance. A few theorists have addressed the spiritual dimension—how deeper values and a sense of purpose influence performance. Almost no one has paid any attention to the role played by physical capacities. A successful approach to sustained high performance, we have found, must pull together all of these elements and consider the person as a whole. Thus, our integrated theory of performance management addresses the body, the emotions, the mind, and the spirit. We call this hierarchy the *performance pyramid* (see the exhibit entitled "The High-Performance Pyramid.") Each of its levels profoundly influences the others, and failure to address any one of them compromises performance.

Our approach has its roots in the two decades that Jim Loehr and his colleagues at LGE spent working with world-class athletes. Several years ago, the two of us began to develop a more comprehensive version of these techniques for executives facing unprecedented demands in the workplace. In effect, we realized, these executives are "corporate athletes." If they were to perform at high levels over the long haul, we posited, they would have to train in the same systematic, multilevel way that world-class athletes do. We have now tested our model on thousands of executives. Their dramatically improved work performance and their enhanced health and happiness confirm our initial hypothesis. In the pages that follow, we describe our approach in detail.

Ideal Performance State

In training athletes, we have never focused on their primary skills—how to hit a serve, swing a golf club, or shoot a basketball. Likewise, in business we don't address primary competencies such as public speaking, negotiating, or analyzing a balance sheet. Our efforts aim instead to help executives build their capacity for what might be called supportive or secondary competencies, among them endurance, strength, flexibility, self-control, and focus. Increasing capacity at all levels allows athletes and executives alike to bring their talents and skills to full ignition and to sustain high performance over time—a condition we call the *Ideal Performance State* (IPS). Obviously, executives can perform successfully even if they smoke, drink and weigh too much, or lack emotional skills or a higher purpose for working. But they cannot perform to their full potential or without a cost over time—to themselves, to their families, and to the corporations for which they work. Put simply, the best long-term performers tap into positive energy at all levels of the performance pyramid.

Extensive research in sports science has confirmed that the capacity to mobilize energy on demand is the foundation of IPS. Our own work has demonstrated that effective energy management has two key components. The first is the rhythmic movement between energy expenditure (stress) and energy renewal (recovery), which we term "oscillation." In the living laboratory of sports, we learned that the real enemy of high performance is not stress, which, paradoxical as it may seem, is actually the stimulus for growth. Rather, the problem is the absence of disciplined, intermittent recovery. Chronic stress without recovery depletes energy reserves, leads to burnout and breakdown, and ultimately undermines performance.

Rituals that promote oscillation—rhythmic stress and recovery—are the second component of high performance. Repeated regularly, these highly precise, consciously developed routines become automatic over time.

The same methods that enable world-class athletes to reach IPS under pressure, we theorized, would be at least

---

The High-Performance Pyramid

Peak performance in business has often been presented as a matter of sheer brainpower, but we view performance as a pyramid. Physical well-being is its foundation. Above that rests emotional health, then mental acuity, and at the top, a sense of purpose. The Ideal Performance State— peak performance under pressure—is achieved when all levels are working together.

Rituals that promote oscillation—the rhythmic expenditure and recovery of energy—link the levels of the pyramid. For instance, vigorous exercise can produce a sense of emotional well-being, clearing the way for peak mental performance.

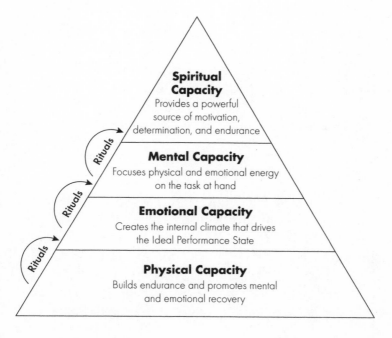

Spiritual Capacity
Provides a powerful source of motivation, determination, and endurance

Mental Capacity
Focuses physical and emotional energy on the task at hand

Emotional Capacity
Creates the internal climate that drives the Ideal Performance State

Physical Capacity
Builds endurance and promotes mental and emotional recovery

Rituals *Rituals* *Rituals*

equally effective for business leaders—and perhaps even more important in their lives. The demands on executives to sustain high performance day in and day out, year in and year out, dwarf the challenges faced by any athlete we have ever trained. The average professional athlete, for example, spends most of his time practicing and only a small percentage—several hours a day, at most—actually competing. The typical executive, by contrast, devotes almost no time to training and must perform on demand ten, 12, 14 hours a day or more. Athletes enjoy several months of off-season, while most executives are fortunate to get three or four weeks of vacation a year. The career of the average professional athlete spans seven years; the average executive can expect to work 40 to 50 years.

Of course, even corporate athletes who train at all levels will have bad days and run into challenges they can't overcome. Life is tough, and for many time-starved executives, it is only getting tougher. But that is precisely our point. While it isn't always in our power to change our external conditions, we can train to better manage our inner state. We aim to help corporate athletes use the full range of their capacities to thrive in the most difficult circumstances and to emerge from stressful periods stronger, healthier, and eager for the next challenge.

Physical Capacity

Energy can be defined most simply as the capacity to do work. Our training process begins at the physical level because the body is our fundamental source of energy—the foundation of the performance pyramid. Perhaps the best paradigm for building capacity is weight lifting. Several decades of sports science research have established that the key to increasing physical strength is a phenomenon known as supercompensation—essentially the creation of balanced work-rest ratios. In weight lifting, this involves stressing a muscle to the point where its fibers literally start to break down. Given an adequate period of recovery (typically at least 48 hours), the muscle will not only heal, it will grow stronger. But persist in stressing the muscle without rest and the result will be acute and chronic damage. Conversely, failure to stress the muscle results in weakness and atrophy. (Just think of an arm in a cast for several weeks.) In both cases, the enemy is not stress, it's linearity—the failure to oscillate between energy expenditure and recovery.

We first understood the power of rituals to prompt recovery by observing world-class tennis players in the crucible of match play. The best competitors, we discovered, use precise recovery rituals in the 15 or 20 seconds *between* points—often without even being aware of it. Their between-point routines include concentrating on the strings of their rackets to avoid distraction, assuming a confident posture, and visualizing how they want the next point to play out. These routines have startling physiological effects. When we hooked players up to heart rate monitors during their matches, the competitors with the most consistent rituals showed dramatic oscillation, their heart rates rising rapidly during play and then dropping as much as 15% to 20% between points.

The mental and emotional effects of precise between-point routines are equally significant. They allow players to avoid negative feelings, focus their minds, and prepare for the next point. By contrast, players who lack between-point rituals, or who practice them inconsistently, become linear—they expend too much energy without recovery. Regardless of their talent or level of fitness, they become more vulnerable to frustration, anxiety, and loss of concentration and far more likely to choke under pressure.

The same lesson applies to the corporate athletes we train. The problem, we explain, is not so much that their lives are increasingly stressful as that they are so relentlessly linear. Typically, they push themselves too hard mentally and emotionally and too little physically. Both forms of linearity undermine performance.

When we began working with Marilyn Clark, a managing director of Salomon Smith Barney, she had almost no oscillation in her life. Clark, who is in her late 30s, runs the firm's Cleveland office. She is also the mother of three young children, and her husband is a high-powered executive in his own right. To all appearances, Clark lives an enviable life, and she was loath to complain about it. Yet her hectic lifestyle was exacting a cost, which became clear after some probing. In the mornings, temporarily fueled by coffee and a muffin, she was alert and energetic. By the afternoon, though, her energy sagged, and she got through the rest of the day on sheer willpower. At lunchtime, when she could have taken a few quiet moments to recover, she found that she couldn't say no to employees who lined up at her office seeking counsel and support. Between the demands of her job, her colleagues, and her family, she had almost no time for herself. Her frustration quietly grew.

We began our work with Clark by taking stock of her physical capacity. While she had been a passionate athlete as a teenager and an All-American lacrosse player in college, her fitness regimen for the past several years had been limited to occasional sit-ups before bedtime. As she learned more about the relationship between energy and high performance, Clark agreed that her first priority was to get back in shape. She wanted to feel better physically, and she knew from past experience that her mood would improve if she built regular workouts into her schedule.

Because old habits die hard, we helped Clark establish positive rituals to replace them. Part of the work was creating a supportive environment. The colleagues with whom Clark trained became a source of cheerleading— and even nagging—as she established a routine that would have previously seemed unthinkable. Clark committed to work out in a nearby gym three days a week, precisely at 1 PM. She also enlisted her husband to watch the kids so that she could get in a workout on Saturdays and Sundays.

Regular workouts have helped Clark create clear work-life boundaries and restored her sense of herself as an athlete. Now, rather than tumbling into an energy trough in the afternoons and reaching for a candy bar, Clark returns to the office from her workouts feeling reenergized and better able to focus. Physical stress has become a source not just of greater endurance but also of emotional and mental recovery; Clark finds that she can work fewer hours and get more done. And finally, because she no longer feels chronically overburdened, she believes that she has become a better boss. "My body feels reawakened," she says. "I'm much more relaxed, and the resentment I was feeling about all the demands on me is gone."

Clark has inspired other members of her firm to take out health club memberships. She and several colleagues are subsidizing employees who can't easily afford the cost. "We're not just talking to each other about business accolades and who is covering which account," she says. "Now it's also about whether we got our workouts in and how well we're recovering. We're sharing something healthy, and that has brought people together."

The corporate athlete doesn't build a strong physical foundation by exercise alone, of course. Good sleeping and eating rituals are integral to effective energy management. When we first met Rudy Borneo, the vice chairman of Macy's West, he complained of erratic energy levels, wide mood swings, and difficulty concentrating. He was also overweight. Like many executives—and most Americans—his eating habits were poor. He typically began his long, travel-crammed days by skipping breakfast—the equivalent of rolling to the start line of the Indianapolis 500 with a near-empty fuel tank. Lunch was catch-as-catch-can, and Borneo used sugary snacks to fight off his inevitable afternoon hunger pangs. These foods spiked his blood glucose levels, giving him a quick jolt of energy, but one that faded quickly. Dinner was often a rich, multicourse meal eaten late in the evening. Digesting that much food disturbed Borneo's sleep and left him feeling sluggish and out of sorts in the mornings.

Sound familiar?

As we did with Clark, we helped Borneo replace his bad habits with positive rituals, beginning with the way he ate. We explained that by eating lightly but often, he could sustain a steady level of energy. (For a fuller account of the foundational exercise, eating, and sleep routines, see the insert "A Firm Foundation" at the end of this article.) Borneo now eats breakfast every day—typically a high-protein drink rather than coffee and a bagel. We also showed him research by chronobiologists suggesting that the body and mind need recovery every 90 to 120 minutes. Using that cycle as the basis for his eating schedule, he installed a refrigerator by his desk and began eating five or six small but nutritious meals a day and sipping water frequently. He also shifted the emphasis in his workouts to interval training, which increased his endurance and speed of recovery.

In addition to prompting weight loss and making him feel better, Borneo's nutritional and fitness rituals have had a dramatic effect on other aspects of his life. "I now exercise for my mind as much as for my body," he says. "At the age of 59, I have more energy than ever, and I can sustain it for a longer period of time. For me, the rituals are the holy grail. Using them to create balance has had an impact on every aspect of my life: staying more positive, handling difficult human resource issues, dealing with change, treating people better. I really do believe that when you learn to take care of yourself, you free up energy and enthusiasm to care more for others."

Emotional Capacity

The next building block of IPS is emotional capacity— the internal climate that supports peak performance. During our early research, we asked hundreds of athletes to describe how they felt when they were performing at their best. Invariably, they used words such as "calm," "challenged," "engaged," "focused," "optimistic," and "confident." As sprinter Marion Jones put it shortly after winning one of her gold medals at the Olympic Games in Sydney: "I'm out here having a ball. This is not a stressful time in my life. This is a very happy time." When we later asked the same question of law enforcement officers, military personnel, surgeons, and corporate executives, they used remarkably similar language to describe their Ideal Performance State.

Just as positive emotions ignite the energy that drives high performance, negative emotions—frustration, impatience, anger, fear, resentment, and sadness—drain energy. Over time, these feelings can be literally toxic, elevating heart rate and blood pressure, increasing muscle tension, constricting vision, and ultimately crippling performance. Anxious, fear ridden athletes are far more likely to choke in competition, for example, while anger and frustration sabotage their capacity for calm focus.

The impact of negative emotions on business performance is subtler but no less devastating. Alan, an executive at an investment company, travels frequently, overseeing a half-dozen offices around the country. His colleagues and subordinates, we learned, considered him to be a perfectionist and an often critical boss whose frustration and impatience sometimes boiled over into angry tirades. Our work focused on helping Alan find ways to manage his emotions more effectively. His anger, we explained, was a reactive emotion, a fight-or-flight response to situations he perceived as threatening. To manage more effectively, he needed to transform his inner experience of threat under stress into one of challenge.

A regular workout regimen built Alan's endurance and gave him a way to burn off tension. But because his fierce travel schedule often got in the way of his workouts, we also helped him develop a precise five-step ritual to contain his negative emotions whenever they threatened to erupt. His initial challenge was to become more aware of signals from his body that he was on edge—physical tension, a racing heart, tightness in his chest. When he felt those sensations arise, his first step was to close his eyes and take several deep breaths. Next, he consciously relaxed the muscles in his face. Then, he made an effort to soften his voice and speak more slowly. After that, he tried to put himself in the shoes of the person who was the target of his anger—to imagine what he or she must be feeling. Finally, he focused on framing his response in positive language.

Instituting this ritual felt awkward to Alan at first, not unlike trying to learn a new golf swing. More than once he reverted to his old behavior. But within several weeks, the five-step drill had become automatic—a highly reliable way to short-circuit his reactivity. Numerous employees reported that he had become more reasonable, more approachable, and less scary. Alan himself says that he has become a far more effective manager.

Through our work with athletes, we have learned a number of other rituals that help to offset feelings of stress and restore positive energy. It's no coincidence, for example, that many athletes wear headphones as they prepare for competition. Music has powerful physiological and emotional effects. It can prompt a shift in mental activity from the rational left hemisphere of the brain to the more intuitive right hemisphere. It also provides a relief from obsessive thinking and worrying. Finally, music can be a means of directly regulating energy—raising it when the time comes to perform and lowering it when it is more appropriate to decompress.

Body language also influences emotions. In one well-known experiment, actors were asked to portray anger and then were subjected to numerous physiological tests, including heart rate, blood pressure, core temperature, galvanic skin response, and hormone levels. Next, the actors were exposed to a situation that made them genuinely angry, and the same measurements were taken. There were virtually no differences in the two profiles. Effective acting produces precisely the same physiology that real emotions do. All great athletes understand this instinctively. If they carry themselves confidently, they will eventually start to feel confident, even in highly stressful situations. That's why we train our corporate clients to "act as if"—consciously creating the look on the outside that they want to feel on the inside. "You are what you repeatedly do," said Aristotle. "Excellence is not a singular act but a habit."

Close relationships are perhaps the most powerful means for prompting positive emotions and effective recovery. Anyone who has enjoyed a happy family reunion or an evening with good friends knows the profound sense of safety and security that these relationships can induce. Such feelings are closely associated with the Ideal Performance State. Unfortunately, many of the corporate athletes we train believe that in order to perform up to expectations at work, they have no choice but to stint on their time with loved ones. We try to reframe the issue. By devoting more time to their most important relationships and setting clearer boundaries between work and home, we tell our clients, they will not only derive more satisfaction but will also get the recovery that they need to perform better at work.

Mental Capacity

The third level of the performance pyramid—the cognitive—is where most traditional performance-enhancement training is aimed. The usual approaches tend to focus on improving competencies by using techniques such as process reengineering and knowledge management or by learning to use more sophisticated technology. Our training aims to enhance our clients' cognitive capacities—most notably their focus, time management, and positive- and critical-thinking skills.

Focus simply means energy concentrated in the service of a particular goal. Anything that interferes with focus dissipates energy. Meditation, typically viewed as a spiritual practice, can serve as a highly practical means of training attention and promoting recovery. At this level, no guidance from a guru is required. A perfectly adequate meditation technique involves sitting quietly and breathing deeply, counting each exhalation, and starting over when you reach ten. Alternatively, you can choose a word to repeat each time you take a breath.

Practiced regularly, meditation quiets the mind, the emotions, and the body, promoting energy recovery. Numerous studies have shown, for example, that experienced meditators need considerably fewer hours of sleep than nonmeditators. Meditation and other noncognitive disciplines can also slow brain wave activity and stimulate a shift in mental activity from the left hemisphere of the brain to the right. Have you ever suddenly found the solution to a vexing problem while doing something "mindless" such as jogging, working in the garden, or singing in the shower? That's the left-brain, right-brain shift at work—the fruit of mental oscillation.

Much of our training at this level focuses on helping corporate athletes to consciously manage their time and energy. By alternating periods of stress with renewal, they learn to align their work with the body's need for breaks every 90 to 120 minutes. This can be challenging for compulsive corporate achievers. Jeffrey Sklar, 39, managing director for institutional sales at the New York investment firm Gruntal & Company, had long been accustomed to topping his competitors by brute force— pushing harder and more relentlessly than anyone else. With our help, he built a set of rituals that ensured regular recovery and also enabled him to perform at a higher level while spending fewer hours at work.

Once in the morning and again in the afternoon, Sklar retreats from the frenetic trading floor to a quiet office, where he spends 15 minutes doing deep-breathing exercises. At lunch, he leaves the office—something he once would have found unthinkable—and walks outdoors for at least 15 minutes. He also works out five or six times a week after work. At home, he and his wife, Sherry, a busy executive herself, made a pact never to talk business after 8 PM. They also swore off work on the weekends, and they have stuck to their vow for nearly two years. During each of those years, Sklar's earnings have increased by more than 65%.

For Jim Connor, the president and CEO of FootJoy, reprioritizing his time became a way not just to manage his energy better but to create more balance in his life and to revive his sense of passion. Connor had come to us saying that he felt stuck in a deep rut. "My feelings were muted so I could deal with the emotional pain of life," he explains. "I had smoothed out all the vicissitudes in my life to such an extent that oscillation was prohibited. I was not feeling life but repetitively performing it."

Connor had imposed on himself the stricture that he be the first person to arrive at the office each day and the last to leave. In reality, he acknowledged, no one would object if he arrived a little later or left a little earlier a couple of days a week. He realized it also made sense for him to spend one or two days a week working at a satellite plant 45 minutes nearer to his home than his main office. Doing so could boost morale at the second plant while cutting 90 minutes from his commute.

Immediately after working with us, Connor arranged to have an office cleared out at the satellite factory. He now spends at least one full day a week there, prompting a number of people at that office to comment to him about his increased availability. He began taking a golf lesson one morning a week, which also allowed for a more relaxed drive to his main office, since he commutes there after rush hour on golf days. In addition, he instituted a monthly getaway routine with his wife. In the evenings, he often leaves his office earlier in order to spend more time with his family.

Connor has also meticulously built recovery into his workdays. "What a difference these fruit and water breaks make," he says. "I set my alarm watch for 90 minutes to prevent relapses, but I'm instinctively incorporating this routine into my life and love it. I'm far more productive as a result, and the quality of my thought process is measurably improved. I'm also doing more on the big things at work and not getting bogged down in detail. I'm pausing more to think and to take time out."

Rituals that encourage positive thinking also increase the likelihood of accessing the Ideal Performance State. Once again, our work with top athletes has taught us the power of creating specific mental rituals to sustain positive energy. Jack Nicklaus, one of the greatest pressure performers in the history of golf, seems to have an intuitive understanding of the importance of both oscillation and rituals. "I've developed a regimen that allows me to move from peaks of concentration into valleys of relaxation and back again as necessary," he wrote in *Golf Digest*. "My focus begins to sharpen as I walk onto the tee and steadily intensifies . . . until I hit [my drive]. . . . I descend into a valley as I leave the tee, either through casual conversation with a fellow competitor or by letting my mind dwell on whatever happens into it."

Visualization is another ritual that produces positive energy and has palpable performance results. For example, Earl Woods taught his son Tiger—Nicklaus's heir apparent—to form a mental image of the ball rolling into the hole before each shot. The exercise does more than produce a vague feeling of optimism and well-being. Neuroscientist Ian Robertson of Trinity College, Dublin, author of *Mind Sculpture,* has found that visualization can literally reprogram the neural circuitry of the brain, directly improving performance. It is hard to imagine a better illustration than diver Laura Wilkinson. Six months before the summer Olympics in Sydney, Wilkinson broke three toes on her right foot while training. Unable to go in the water because of her cast, she instead spent hours a day on the diving platform, visualizing each of her dives. With only a few weeks to actually practice before the Olympics, she pulled off a huge upset, winning the gold medal on the ten-meter platform.

Visualization works just as well in the office. Sherry Sklar has a ritual to prepare for any significant event in her work life. "I always take time to sit down in advance in a quiet place and think about what I really want from the meeting," she says. "Then I visualize myself achieving the outcome I'm after." In effect, Sklar is building mental muscles—increasing her strength, endurance, and flexibility. By doing so, she decreases the likelihood that she will be distracted by negative thoughts under pressure. "It has made me much more relaxed and confident when I go into presentations," she says.

Spiritual Capacity

Most executives are wary of addressing the spiritual level of the performance pyramid in business settings, and understandably so. The word "spiritual" prompts conflicting emotions and doesn't seem immediately relevant to high performance. So let's be clear: by spiritual

capacity, we simply mean the energy that is unleashed
by tapping into one's deepest values and defining a
strong sense of purpose. This capacity, we have found,
serves as sustenance in the face of adversity and as a
powerful source of motivation, focus, determination,
and resilience.

Consider the case of Ann, a high-level executive at a
large cosmetics company. For much of her adult life, she
has tried unsuccessfully to quit smoking, blaming her
failures on a lack of self-discipline. Smoking took a visible toll on her health and her productivity at work—
decreased endurance from shortness of breath, more sick
days than her colleagues, and nicotine cravings that distracted her during long meetings.

Four years ago, when Ann became pregnant, she was
able to quit immediately and didn't touch a cigarette
until the day her child was born, when she began smoking again. A year later, Ann became pregnant for a second time, and again she stopped smoking, with virtually
no symptoms of withdrawal. True to her pattern, she
resumed smoking when her child was born. "I don't
understand it," she told us plaintively.

We offered a simple explanation. As long as Ann was
able to connect the impact of smoking to a deeper purpose—the health of her unborn child—quitting was easy.
She was able to make what we call a "values-based adaptation." But without a strong connection to a deeper
sense of purpose, she went back to smoking—an expedi-
ent adaptation that served her short-term interests.
Smoking was a sensory pleasure for Ann, as well as a way
to allay her anxiety and manage social stress. Understanding cognitively that it was unhealthy, feeling guilty
about it on an emotional level, and even experiencing its

negative effects physically were all insufficient motivations to change her behavior. To succeed, Ann needed a more sustaining source of motivation.

Making such a connection, we have found, requires regularly stepping off the endless treadmill of deadlines and obligations to take time for reflection. The inclination for busy executives is to live in a perpetual state of triage, doing whatever seems most immediately pressing while losing sight of any bigger picture. Rituals that give people the opportunity to pause and look inside include meditation, journal writing, prayer, and service to others. Each of these activities can also serve as a source of recovery—a way to break the linearity of relentless goal-oriented activity.

Taking the time to connect to one's deepest values can be extremely rewarding. It can also be painful, as a client we'll call Richard discovered. Richard is a stockbroker who works in New York City and lives in a distant suburb, where his wife stays at home with their three young children. Between his long commute and his long hours, Richard spent little time with his family. Like so many of our clients, he typically left home before his children woke up and returned around 7:30 in the evening, feeling exhausted and in no mood to talk to anyone. He wasn't happy with his situation, but he saw no easy solution. In time, his unhappiness began to affect his work, which made him even more negative when he got home at night. It was a vicious cycle.

One evening while driving home from work, Richard found himself brooding about his life. Suddenly, he felt so overcome by emotion that he stopped his car at a park ten blocks from home to collect himself. To his astonishment, he began to weep. He felt consumed with grief about his life and filled with longing for his family. After ten minutes, all Richard wanted to do was get home and hug his wife and children. Accustomed to giving their dad a wide berth at the end of the day, his kids were understandably bewildered when he walked in that evening with tears streaming down his face and wrapped them all in hugs. When his wife arrived on the scene, her first thought was that he'd been fired.

The next day, Richard again felt oddly compelled to stop at the park near his house. Sure enough, the tears returned and so did the longing. Once again, he rushed home to his family. During the subsequent two years, Richard was able to count on one hand the number of times that he failed to stop at the same location for at least ten minutes. The rush of emotion subsided over time, but his sense that he was affirming what mattered most in his life remained as strong as ever.

Richard had stumbled into a ritual that allowed him both to disengage from work and to tap into a profound source of purpose and meaning—his family. In that context, going home ceased to be a burden after a long day and became instead a source of recovery and renewal. In turn, Richard's distraction at work diminished, and he became more focused, positive, and productive—so much so that he was able to cut down on his hours. On a practical level, he created a better balance between stress and recovery. Finally, by tapping into a deeper sense of purpose, he found a powerful new source of energy for both his work and his family.

In a corporate environment that is changing at warp speed, performing consistently at high levels is more difficult and more necessary than ever. Narrow interventions simply aren't sufficient anymore. Companies can't afford to address their employees' cognitive capacities while ignoring their physical, emotional, and spiritual well-being. On the playing field or in the boardroom, high performance depends as much on how people renew and recover energy as on how they expend it, on how they manage their lives as much as on how they manage their work. When people feel strong and resilient—physically, mentally, emotionally, and spiritually—they perform better, with more passion, for longer. They win, their families win, and the corporations that employ them win.

A Firm Foundation

HERE ARE OUR BASIC STRATEGIES for renewing energy at the physical level. Some of them are so familiar they've become background noise, easy to ignore. That's why we're repeating them. If any of these strategies aren't part of your life now, their absence may help account for fatigue, irritability, lack of emotional resilience, difficulty concentrating, and even a flagging sense of purpose.

1. **Actually do all those healthy things you know you ought to do.** Eat five or six small meals a day; people who eat just one or two meals a day with long periods in between force their bodies into a conservation mode, which translates into slower metabolism. Always eat breakfast: eating first thing in the morning sends your body the signal that it need not slow metabolism to conserve energy. Eat a balanced diet. Despite all the conflicting nutritional research, overwhelming evidence suggests that a healthy dietary ratio is 50% to 60% complex

carbohydrates, 25% to 35% protein, and 20% to 25% fat. Dramatically reduce simple sugars. In addition to representing empty calories, sugar causes energy-depleting spikes in blood glucose levels. Drink four to five 12-ounce glasses of water daily, even if you don't feel thirsty. As much as half the population walks around with mild chronic dehydration. And finally, on the "you know you should" list: get physically active. We strongly recommend three to four 20- to 30-minute cardiovascular workouts a week, including at least two sessions of intervals—short bursts of intense exertion followed by brief recovery periods.

2. **Go to bed early and wake up early.** Night owls have a much more difficult time dealing with the demands of today's business world, because typically, they still have to get up with the early birds. They're often groggy and unfocused in the mornings, dependent on caffeine and sugary snacks to keep up their energy. You can establish new sleep rituals. Biological clocks are not fixed in our genes.

3. **Maintain a consistent bedtime and wake-up time.** As important as the number of hours you sleep (ideally seven to eight) is the consistency of the recovery wave you create. Regular sleep cycles help regulate your other biological clocks and increase the likelihood that the sleep you get will be deep and restful.

4. **Seek recovery every 90 to 120 minutes.** Chronobiologists have found that the body's hormone, glucose, and blood pressure levels drop every 90 minutes or so. By failing to seek recovery and overriding the body's natural stress-rest cycles, overall capacity is compromised. As we've learned from athletes, even short, focused breaks can promote significant recovery. We suggest five

sources of restoration: eat something, hydrate, move physically, change channels mentally, and change channels emotionally.

5. **Do at least two weight-training workouts a week.** No form of exercise more powerfully turns back the markers of age than weight training. It increases strength, retards osteoporosis, speeds up metabolism, enhances mobility, improves posture, and dramatically increases energy.

Originally published in January 2001
Reprint R0101H

Are You Working Too Hard?

A CONVERSATION WITH

HERBERT BENSON, MD

Executive Summary

STRESS IS AN ESSENTIAL RESPONSE in highly competitive environments. Before a race, before an exam, before an important meeting, your heart rate and blood pressure rise, your focus tightens, you become more alert and more efficient. But beyond a certain level, stress overloads your system, compromising your performance and, eventually, your health.

So the question is: When does stress help and when does it hurt? To find out, HBR talked with Harvard Medical School professor Herbert Benson, MD, founder of the Mind/Body Medical Institute. Having spent more than 35 years conducting worldwide research in the fields of neuroscience and stress, Benson is best known for his 1975 best seller *The Relaxation Response*, in which he describes how the mind can influence stress levels through such tools as meditation. His most recent

research centers on what he calls "the breakout principle," a method by which stress is not simply reduced but
carefully controlled so that you reap its benefits while
avoiding its dangers. He describes a four-step process in
which you first push yourself to the most productive stress
level by grappling intently with a problem. Next, just as
you feel yourself flagging, you disengage entirely by
doing something utterly unrelated—going for a walk, pet-
ting a dog, taking a shower. In the third step, as the brain
quiets down, activity paradoxically increases in areas
associated with attention, space-time concepts, and decision making, leading to a sudden, creative insight—the
breakout. Step four is achievement of a "new-normal
state," in which you find that the improved performance
is sustained, sometimes indefinitely.

As counterintuitive as this research may seem, managers can doubtless recall times when they've had
an "aha" moment at the gym, on the golf course, or
in the shower. What Benson describes here is a way
to tap into this invaluable biological tool whenever
we want.

---

*Managers apply pressure to themselves and their teams
in the belief that it will make them more productive. After
all, stress is an intrinsic part of work and a critical ele-
ment of achievement; without a certain amount of it, we
would never perform at all.*

*Yet the dangers of burnout are real. Studies cited by
the National Institute for Occupational Safety and Health
(NIOSH) indicate that some 40% of all workers today
feel overworked, pressured, and squeezed to the point
of anxiety, depression, and disease. And the problem is*

getting worse, thanks to intensified competition, rapid market changes, and an unending stream of terrible news about natural disasters, terrorism, and the state of the economy. The cost to employers is appalling: Corporate health insurance premiums in the United States shot up by 11.2% in 2004—quadruple the rate of inflation— according to survey figures from the Henry J. Kaiser Family Foundation. Today, the American Institute of Stress reports, roughly 60% of doctor visits stem from stress-related complaints and illnesses: In total, American businesses lose $300 billion annually to lowered productivity, absenteeism, health-care, and related costs stemming from stress.

So the question is: When does stress help and when does it hurt? To find out, HBR senior editor Bronwyn Fryer talked with Herbert Benson, MD, founder of the Mind/Body Medical Institute in Chestnut Hill, Massachusetts. Also an associate professor of medicine at Harvard Medical School, Benson has spent more than 35 years conducting research in the fields of neuroscience and stress. He is best known for his 1975 best seller, The Relaxation Response. He first described a technique to bring forth the complex physiologic dance between stress and relaxation, and the benefits to managers of practices such as meditation, in "Your Innate Asset for Combating Stress" (HBR July–August 1974). His most recent book is The Breakout Principle (Scribner, 2003) with William Proctor.

Benson and Proctor have found that managers can learn to use stress productively by applying the "breakout principle"—a paradoxical active-passive dynamic. By using simple techniques to regulate the amounts of stress one feels, a manager can increase performance and productivity and avoid burnout. In this edited conversation,

Benson describes how managers can tap into their own creative insights, boost their productivity at work, and assist their teams to do the same. He is quick to acknowledge the large part Proctor's thinking has played in the ideas he discusses here.

We all know that unmanaged stress can be destructive. But are there positive sides to stress as well?

Yes, but let's define what stress is first. Stress is a physiological response to any change, whether good or bad, that alerts the adaptive fight-or-flight response in the brain and the body. Good stress, also called "eustress," gives us energy and motivates us to strive and produce. We see eustress in elite athletes, creative artists, and all kinds of high achievers. Anyone who's clinched an important deal or had a good performance review, for example, enjoys the benefits of eustress, such as clear thinking, focus, and creative insight.

But when most people talk about stress, they are referring to the bad kind. At work, negative stressors are usually the perceived actions of customers, clients, bosses, colleagues, and employees, combined with demanding deadlines. At the Mind/Body Medical Institute, we also encounter executives who worry incessantly about Sarbanes-Oxley compliance, the impact of China on their companies' markets, the state of the economy, the world oil supply, and so on. Additionally, people bring to work the stress aroused by dealing with family problems, taxes, and traffic jams, as well as anxieties stemming from a continuous diet of bad news that upsets them and makes them feel helpless—hurricanes, politics, child abductions, wars, terrorist attacks, environmental devastation, you name it.

Many companies offer various kinds of stress-reduction programs, from on-site yoga classes and massage to fancy gyms to workshops. What's wrong with these?

It's critical that companies do something to address the rampant negative effects of workplace stress if they want to compete effectively, but often the kinds of programs they institute are stopgaps. HR may bring in a lecturer once or twice a year or set up tai chi sessions and urge everyone to go, but few people show up because they feel they can't take the time to eat their lunch, much less spend an hour doing something perceived as both unrelated to work and relaxing to boot. Unless the leadership and culture explicitly encourage people to join in, employees will continue to feel guilty or worry that they'll be seen as slackers if they go.

This state of affairs is inexcusable if you look at the billions lost to absenteeism, turnover, disability, insurance costs, workplace accidents, violence, workers' compensation, and lawsuits, not to mention the expense of replacing valuable employees lost to stress-related problems. Fortunately, each of us holds the key for managing stress, and leaders who learn to do this and help their employees to do likewise can tap into enormous productivity and potential while mitigating these costs.

What is the science behind your latest research, and what does it reveal?

First, let me say that we at the Mind/Body Medical Institute didn't discover anything new. The American philosopher William James identified the breakout principle in his *Varieties of Religious Experience* in 1902. What we set about to do was explore the science behind what James had identified.

Over the past 35 years, our teams have collected data on thousands of subjects from population studies, physiologic measurements, brain imaging, molecular biology, biochemistry, and other approaches to measuring bodily reactions to stress. From these we identified the relaxation response and could see how powerful it was. It is a physical state of deep rest that counteracts the harmful effects of the fight-or-flight response, such as increased heart rate, blood pressure, and muscle tension.

Neurologically, what happens is this: When we encounter a stressor at work—a difficult employee, a tough negotiation, a tight deadline, or worse—we can deal with it for a little while before the negative effects set in. But if we are exposed for excessively long periods to the fight-or-flight response, the pressure on us will become too great, and our system will be flooded with the hormones epinephrine, norepinephrine, and cortisol. These cause blood pressure to rise and the heart rate and brain activity to increase, effects that are very deleterious over time. But our latest findings indicate that by completely letting go of a problem at that point by applying certain triggers, the brain actually rearranges itself so that the hemispheres communicate better. Then the brain is better able to solve the problem.

The best way to understand this mechanism is to go back nearly 100 years to the work of two Harvard researchers, Robert Yerkes and John Dodson. In 1908, these two demonstrated that efficiency increases when stress increases, but only up to a point; after that, performance falls off dramatically (see the exhibit "The Yerkes-Dodson Curve"). We found that by taking the stress level up to the top of the bell curve and then effectively pulling the rug out from under it by turning to a quieting, rejuvenating activity, subjects could evoke the relaxation response, which effectively counteracts the negative effects of the stress hormones. Molecular studies have shown that the calming response releases little "puffs" of nitric oxide, which has been linked to the production of such neurotransmitters as endorphins and dopamine. These chemicals enhance general feelings of well-being. As the brain quiets down, another phenomenon that we call "calm commotion"— or a focused increase in activity—takes place in the areas of the brain associated with attention, space-time concepts, and decision making.

In eliciting the relaxation response, individuals experience a sudden creative insight, in which the solution to the problem becomes apparent. This is a momentary phenomenon. Thereafter, the subjects enter a state of

---

The Yerkes-Dodson Curve

Stress is an essential response in highly competitive environments. Before a race, before an exam, before an important meeting, your heart rate goes up and so does your blood pressure. You become more focused, alert, and efficient. But past a certain level, stress compromises your performance, efficiency, and eventually your health. Two Harvard researchers, Robert M. Yerkes and John D. Dodson, first calibrated the relationship between stress and performance in 1908, which has been dubbed the Yerkes-Dodson law.

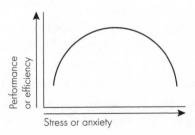

sustained improved performance, which we call the
"new-normal" state, because the breakthrough effect can
be remembered indefinitely.

We find this to be an intriguing phenomenon. By
bringing the brain to the height of activity and then suddenly moving it into a passive, relaxed state, it's possible
to stimulate much higher neurological performance than
would otherwise be the case. Over time, subjects who
learn to do this as a matter of course perform at consistently higher levels. The effect is particularly noticeable
in athletes and creative artists, but we have also seen it
among the businesspeople we work with.

So how would a manager actually go about tapping into the breakout principle?

A breakout sequence occurs in four steps. The first step
is to struggle mightily with a thorny problem. For a busi-
nessperson, this may be concentrated problem analysis
or fact gathering; it can also simply be thinking intently
about a stressful situation at work—a tough employee, a
performance conundrum, a budgetary difficulty. The key
is to put a significant amount of preliminary hard work
into the matter. Basically, you want to lean into the problem to get to the top of the Yerkes-Dodson curve.

You can tell when you have neared the top of the
curve when you stop feeling productive and start feeling
stressed. You may have unpleasant feelings such as anxiety, fearfulness, anger, or boredom, or you may feel like
procrastinating. You may even have physical symptoms
such as a headache, a knot in the stomach, or sweaty
palms. At this point, it's time to move to step two.

Step two involves walking away from the problem and
doing something utterly different that produces the

relaxation response. There are many ways to do this. A ten-minute relaxation-response exercise, in which you calm your mind and focus on your out-breath while disregarding the thoughts you've been having, works extremely well. Some people go jogging or pet a furry animal; others look at paintings they love. Some relax in a sauna or take a hot shower. Still others "sleep on it" by taking a nap or getting a good night's rest, having a meal with friends, or listening to their favorite calming music. One male executive I know relaxes by doing needlepoint. All of these things bring about the mental rearrangement that is the foundation for new insights, solutions, and creativity. The key is to stop analyzing, surrender control, and completely detach yourself from the stress-producing thoughts. When you allow your brain to quiet down, your body releases the puffs of nitric oxide that make you feel better and make you more productive.

One executive we observed was worried about a big presentation she had to make before some top-level managers. She worked and worked on it, but the harder she worked the more befuddled she became and the more anxiety took over. Fortunately, she had learned to evoke her relaxation response by visiting the art museum near her office. So she did. After a while, she felt a sense of total release as she stood there looking at her favorite pictures. At that point, she suddenly had the insight that she was trying to cover too many topics at once and needed to pare down the presentation to a single, overriding concept she could illustrate with solid examples. She felt inspired and confident that she had the answer. She went back to the office, redid the presentation and, feeling relaxed and happy, went home for the day.

This third step—gaining a sudden insight—is the actual breakout. Breakouts are also often referred to as

"peak experiences," "flow," or "being in the zone." Elite
athletes reach this state when they train hard and then let
go and allow the muscle memory to take over. They
become completely immersed in what they're doing,
which feels automatic, smooth, and effortless. In all cases,
a breakout is experienced as a sense of well-being and
relaxation that brings with it an unexpected insight or a
higher level of performance. And it's all the result of a simple biological mechanism that we can tap into at will.

The final step is the return to the new-normal state in
which the sense of self-confidence continues. The manager who reorganized her presentation, for example,
came in the next morning knowing all would be well. The
meeting did go well, and she received accolades for her
work from her bosses and colleagues.

Does a breakout occur all the time or just occasionally?
What percentage of people, according to your research,
experience breakouts in this way?

We don't yet have hard data on this, but anecdotally I
can tell you that when you compare groups of people
who have been trained to evoke the relaxation response
to groups who lack such training, the former experience
breakouts much more frequently. About 25% of people
trained in this process, and sometimes many more, can
reliably reach the breakout stage.

Can teams or groups do this together or somehow feed
off one another?

Certainly. The benefits of mind/body management are
by no means limited to individuals. Those who become
skilled in these techniques can also expect to have an

exponential impact in groups or teams; they can work together to solve organizational problems as part of what we might call a mind/body orchestra.

Let me give you an example of how this works. A few years ago, three software executives with whom we had worked spent two days trying to cajole venture capitalists in Singapore to fund several projects having to do with a new kind of encryption technology. They had all thought long and hard about the problems with encryption, both at their home office in the States and in their preparations for the Singapore presentation. This produced significant levels of stress hormones.

After the meetings finally ended, the three of them took a cab to the airport. The drive was long, and they all felt they could finally let their hair down and relax. Through no planning on anyone's part, the environment in the taxi produced the required break from prior thinking patterns and emotions. The sense of relief, the release from days of high stress, the feeling of camaraderie, and the mentally lulling ride in the dark taxi clearly triggered the relaxation response. That put them all in a neurological position to focus and think clearly about encryption.

The inventor of the technology was the most creative thinker of the three, the one who could best integrate his left- and right-brain functions. He tossed out a thought that had just come to him for a revolutionary product. The others, who were more linear and practical in their thinking style, got excited and chimed in with all kinds of questions and ideas for marketing and selling it. By the end of the cab ride, the trio had fashioned an entirely new encryption product—without taking a single note as the final idea emerged in their minds. They filed a provisional patent three weeks afterwards and their final patent application one year later. They are now selling a version of the product as part of a multimillion-dollar enterprise.

Unwinding after a long trip is one thing, but if you were a manager dealing with a project team in a conference room, what might you do to evoke a breakout?

First, I would lay out a picture of an especially difficult project. I'd ask everyone to come to the meeting having thought very hard about their particular task and how that task affects other parts of the project. I would open the meeting by saying something about what we were all trying to achieve.

Then I would tell the group that we want to shift our thinking to produce a breakthrough idea, and we can do that by evoking the relaxation response. When I work with groups of people, I ask them to close their eyes and relax all their muscles, beginning at their feet and progressing up from the feet and legs through the torso, and finally to their shoulders, neck, and head. I ask them to focus on breathing slowly. Every time they breathe out, they should silently say a word or phrase that is personally meaningful to them, like "calm" or "peace." If they happen to be religious, they might say something like the first line of the twenty-third psalm. I instruct them not to worry about what they're doing or what they attach to the thoughts that come into their heads; they should just say to themselves, "oh well," and return to the repetition. This process goes on for about eight to ten minutes. When they finish, they sit quietly with their eyes closed for a minute or so and a moment longer with their eyes open.

After this exercise, they can begin to focus on the assignment. It's very likely that more than one insightful solution will emerge from the group.

It's hard to imagine any leader doing that. It sounds much too soft.

Actually, it's not soft at all. It's a matter of learning to shift our internal biology at will so that we increase production of nitric oxide and the neurotransmitters associated with well-being and increased creativity. And if you think about it, most people experience breakthrough moments at one time or another. Managers can doubtless recall times when they've had an "aha" moment at the gym or on the golf course or in the shower. All I'm saying is that it is possible to leverage this invaluable biological tool when we want or need to.

It sometimes takes a serious illness caused or exacerbated by stress for people to have their "aha" moments. One well-known CEO we worked with spent years putting in more than 60 hours a week at his intensely stressful job. He came to us after he had been diagnosed with a silent heart attack. His world had completely turned upside down. He took a leave of absence from work to focus on healing, to ask himself why he was on the planet, and to spend time with his family. We trained him to use the relaxation response and the breakout principle. He recovered and came back to work far more resilient and productive than he was before.

Ultimately, leaders need only look at the high cost of stress to their businesses to understand why this is so important. They are losing out because they are not paying proper attention to teaching their employees a simple approach—one that can not only save their companies enormous costs but also free the productivity and creativity in their workers.

In the West, we are accustomed to linear thought patterns, which are generally the domain of the left hemisphere of the brain. We excel at technology, science, and analysis. If you are a creative person, you must literally step outside the linear, analytic way of thinking to do your work. This is not so much the case in other cultures, particularly Asian ones, which tend to view things more holistically. In China, for example, thinking is more contextual. If a Westerner gets involved in an argument with a Chinese person, the Westerner will try to gain the upper hand by rationally eliminating contradictions. The Chinese person, by contrast, will incorporate the contradictions and adopt an evolving, less rigid point of view—essentially using both hemispheres of the brain.

Now that you've established the biological basis of the breakout principle, what do you think is the next frontier in mind/body medicine?

It's clear that mind/body medicine is the third leg of a three-legged stool of health and well-being, the other two legs of which are pharmaceuticals and surgery. As people take more responsibility for their own care through diet, exercise, and tools such as the relaxation response, they will become less dependent on the other two legs of the stool.

At the Mind/Body Medical Institute, one frontier is to further demonstrate the applicability of the principle in places where it hasn't been routinely used, especially in the business world. I am convinced that companies that can bring these principles to bear will maximize the brain capabilities of their entire organizations, make them healthier and more productive, and help them compete effectively in this challenging global economy.

Originally published in November 2005
Reprint R0511B

Sleep Deficit

The Performance Killer

A CONVERSATION WITH
HARVARD MEDICAL SCHOOL
PROFESSOR CHARLES A. CZEISLER

Executive Summary

COMPANIES TODAY GLORIFY THE EXECUTIVE who logs 100-hour workweeks, the road warrior who lives out of a suitcase in multiple time zones, and the negotiator who takes a red-eye to make an 8 AM meeting. But to Dr. Charles A. Czeisler, the Baldino Professor of Sleep Medicine at Harvard Medical School, this kind of corporate behavior is the antithesis of high performance. In fact, he says, it endangers employees and puts their companies at risk.

In this interview, Czeisler describes four neurobiological functions that affect sleep duration and quality as well as individual performance. When these functions fall out of alignment because of sleep deprivation, people operate at a far lower level of performance than they would if they were well rested. Czeisler goes on to observe that corporations have all kinds of policies designed to protect employees—rules against smoking, sexual harassment, and so on—but they push people to the brink of self-destruction by expecting them to work too hard, too long, and with too little sleep. The negative effects on cognitive performance, Czeisler says, can be similar to those that occur after drinking too much alcohol: "We now know that 24 hours without sleep or a week of sleeping four or five hours a night induces an impairment equivalent to a blood alcohol level of .1%. We would never say, 'This person is a great worker! He's drunk all the time!' yet we continue to celebrate people who sacrifice sleep for work."

Czeisler recommends that companies institute corporate sleep policies that discourage scheduled work beyond 16 consecutive hours as well as working or driving immediately after late-night or overnight flights. The insert at the end of this article summarizes the latest developments in sleep research.

At 12:30 AM on June 10, 2002, Israel Lane Joubert and his family of seven set out for a long drive home following a family reunion in Beaumont, Texas. Joubert, who had hoped to reach home in faraway Fort Worth in time to get to work by 8 AM, fell asleep at the wheel, plowing the family's Chevy Suburban into the rear of a parked 18-wheeler. He survived, but his wife and five of his six children were killed.

The Joubert tragedy underscores a problem of epidemic proportions among workers who get too little sleep. In the past five years, driver fatigue has accounted for more than 1.35 million automobile accidents in the United States alone, according to the National Highway

Traffic Safety Administration. The general effect of sleep deprivation on cognitive performance is well-known: Stay awake longer than 18 consecutive hours, and your reaction speed, short-term and long-term memory, ability to focus, decision-making capacity, math processing, cognitive speed, and spatial orientation all start to suffer. Cut sleep back to five or six hours a night for several days in a row, and the accumulated sleep deficit magnifies these negative effects. (Sleep deprivation is implicated in all kinds of physical maladies, too, from high blood pressure to obesity.)

Nevertheless, frenzied corporate cultures still confuse sleeplessness with vitality and high performance. An ambitious manager logs 80-hour work weeks, surviving on five or six hours of sleep a night and eight cups of coffee (the world's second-most widely sold commodity, after oil) a day. A Wall Street trader goes to bed at 11 or midnight and wakes to his BlackBerry buzz at 2:30 AM to track opening activity on the DAX. A road warrior lives out of a suitcase while traveling to Tokyo, St. Louis, Miami, and Zurich, conducting business in a cloud of caffeinated jet lag. A negotiator takes a red-eye flight, hops into a rental car, and zooms through an unfamiliar city to make a delicate M&A meeting at 8 in the morning.

People like this put themselves, their teams, their companies, and the general public in serious jeopardy, says Dr. Charles A. Czeisler, the Baldino Professor of Sleep Medicine at Harvard Medical School.[1] To him, encouraging a culture of sleepless machismo is worse than nonsensical; it is downright dangerous, and the antithesis of intelligent management. He notes that while corporations have all kinds of policies designed to prevent employee endangerment—rules against workplace smoking, drinking, drugs, sexual harassment, and so on—they sometimes *push employees to the brink of self-destruction. Being "on" pretty much around the clock induces a level of impairment every bit as risky as intoxication.*

As one of the world's leading authorities on human sleep cycles and the biology of sleep and wakefulness, Dr. Czeisler understands the physiological bases of the sleep imperative better than almost anyone. His message to corporate leaders is simple: If you want to raise per- formance—both your own and your organization's—you need to pay attention to this fundamental biological issue. In this edited interview with senior editor Bronwyn Fryer, Czeisler observes that top executives now have a critical responsibility to take sleeplessness seriously.

What does the most recent research tell us about the physiology of sleep and cognitive performance?

Four major sleep-related factors affect our cognitive performance. The kinds of work and travel schedules required of business executives today pose a severe challenge to their ability to function well, given each of these factors.

The first has to do with the homeostatic drive for sleep at night, determined largely by the number of con- secutive hours that we've been awake. Throughout the waking day, human beings build up a stronger and stronger drive for sleep. Most of us think we're in control of sleep—that we choose when to go to sleep and when to wake up. The fact is that when we are drowsy, the brain can seize control involuntarily. When the homeo- static pressure to sleep becomes high enough, a couple thousand neurons in the brain's "sleep switch" ignite, as discovered by Dr. Clif Saper at Harvard Medical School.

Once that happens, sleep seizes the brain like a pilot grabbing the controls. If you're behind the wheel of a car at the time, it takes just three or four seconds to be off the road.

The second major factor that determines our ability to sustain attention and maintain peak cognitive performance has to do with the total amount of sleep you manage to get over several days. If you get at least eight hours of sleep a night, your level of alertness should remain stable throughout the day, but if you have a sleep disorder or get less than that for several days, you start building a sleep deficit that makes it more difficult for the brain to function. Executives I've observed tend to burn the candle at both ends, with 7 AM breakfast meetings and dinners that run late, for days and days. Most people can't get to sleep without some wind-down time, even if they are very tired, so these executives may not doze off until 2 in the morning. If they average four hours of sleep a night for four or five days, they develop the same level of cognitive impairment as if they'd been awake for 24 hours—equivalent to legal drunkenness. Within ten days, the level of impairment is the same as you'd have going 48 hours without sleep. This greatly lengthens reaction time, impedes judgment, and interferes with problem solving. In such a state of sleep deprivation, a single beer can have the same impact on our ability to sustain performance as a whole six-pack can have on someone who's well rested.

The third factor has to do with the circadian phase— the time of day in the human body that says "it's midnight" or "it's dawn." A neurological timing device called the "circadian pacemaker" works alongside but, paradoxically, in opposition to the homeostatic drive for sleep. This circadian pacemaker sends out its strongest drive for sleep just before we habitually wake up, and its strongest drive for waking one to three hours before we usually go to bed, just when the homeostatic drive for sleep is peaking. We don't know why it's set up this way, but we can speculate that it has to do with the fact that, unlike other animals, we don't take frequent catnaps throughout the day. The circadian pacemaker may help us to focus on that big project by enabling us to stay awake throughout the day in one long interval and by allowing us to consolidate sleep into one long interval at night.

In the midafternoon, when we've already built up substantial homeostatic sleep drive, the circadian system has not yet come to the rescue. That's typically the time when people are tempted to take a nap or head for the closest Starbucks or soda machine. The caffeine in the coffee temporarily blocks receptors in the brain that regulate sleep drive. Thereafter, the circadian pacemaker sends out a stronger and stronger drive for waking as the day progresses. Provided you're keeping a regular schedule, the rise in the sleep-facilitating hormone melatonin will then quiet the circadian pacemaker one to two hours before your habitual bedtime, enabling the homeostatic sleep drive to take over and allow you to get to sleep. As the homeostatic drive dissipates midway through the sleep episode, the circadian drive for sleep increases toward morning, maintaining our ability to obtain a full night of sleep. After our usual wake time, the levels of melatonin begin to decline. Normally, the two mutually opposing processes work well together, sustaining alertness throughout the day and promoting a solid night of sleep.

The fourth factor affecting performance has to do with what's called "sleep inertia," the grogginess most people experience when they first wake up. Just like a car

engine, the brain needs time to "warm up" when you
awaken. The part of your brain responsible for memory
consolidation doesn't function well for five to 20 minutes
after you wake up and doesn't reach its peak efficiency
for a couple of hours. But if you sleep on the airplane and
the flight attendant wakes you up suddenly upon land-
ing, you may find yourself at the customs station before
you realize you've left your laptop and your passport
behind. There is a transitional period between the time
you wake up and the time your brain becomes fully functional. This is why you never want to make an important
decision as soon as you are suddenly awakened—ask
any nurse who's had to awaken a physician at night
about a patient.

*Most top executives are over 40. Isn't it true that sleep-
ing also becomes more difficult with age?*

Yes, that's true. When we're past the age of 40, sleep is
much more fragmented than when we're younger. We are
more easily awakened by disturbances such as noise from
the external environment and from our own increasing
aches and pains. Another thing that increases with age is
the risk of sleep disorders such as restless legs syndrome,
insomnia, and sleep apnea—the cessation of breathing
during sleep, which can occur when the airway collapses
many times per hour and shuts off the flow of oxygen to
the heart and brain, leading to many brief awakenings.

Many people gain weight as they age, too. Interestingly, chronic sleep restriction increases levels of
appetite and stress hormones; it also reduces one's ability to metabolize glucose and increases the production
of the hormone ghrelin, which makes people crave carbohydrates and sugars, so they get heavier, which in turn

raises the risk of sleep apnea, creating a vicious cycle. Some researchers speculate that the epidemic of obesity in the U.S. and elsewhere may be related to chronic sleep loss. Moreover, sleep-disordered breathing increases the risk of high blood pressure and heart disease due to the strain of starving the heart of oxygen many times per hour throughout the night.

As we age, the circadian window during which we maintain consolidated sleep also narrows. That's why airline travel across time zones can be so brutal as we get older. Attempting to sleep at an adverse circadian phase—that is, during our biological daytime—becomes much more difficult. Thus, if you take a 7 PM flight from New York to London, you typically land about midnight in your home time zone, when the homeostatic drive for sleep is very strong, but the local time is 5 AM. Exposure to daylight—the principal circadian synchronizer—at this time shifts you toward Hawaiian time rather than toward London time. In this circumstance, the worst possible thing you can do is rent a car and drive to a meeting where you have to impress people with your mental acuity at the equivalent of 3 or 4 in the morning. You might not even make the meeting, because you very easily could wrap your car around a tree. Fourteen or 15 hours later, if you're trying to go to bed at 11 PM in the local time zone, you'll have a more difficult time maintaining a consolidated night's sleep.

So sleep deprivation, in your opinion, is a far more serious issue than most executives think it is.

Yes, indeed. Putting yourself or others at risk while driving or working at an impaired level is bad enough; expecting your employees to do the same is just irresponsible. It amazes me that contemporary work and social culture glorifies sleeplessness in the way we once glorified people who could hold their liquor. We now know that 24 hours without sleep or a week of sleeping four or five hours a night induces an impairment equivalent to a blood alcohol level of .1%. We would never say, "This person is a great worker! He's drunk all the time!" yet we continue to celebrate people who sacrifice sleep. The analogy to drunkenness is real because, like a drunk, a person who is sleep deprived has no idea how functionally impaired he or she truly is. Moreover, their efficiency at work will suffer substantially, contributing to the phenomenon of "presenteeism," which, as HBR has noted, exacts a large economic toll on business. (See Paul Hemp's article "Presenteeism: At Work—But Out of It," HBR October 2004.)

Sleep deprivation is not just an individual health hazard; it's a public one. Consider the risk of occupational injury and driver fatigue. In a study our research team conducted of hospital interns who had been scheduled to work for at least 24 consecutive hours, we found that their odds of stabbing themselves with a needle or scalpel increased 61%, their risk of crashing a motor vehicle increased 168%, and their risk of a near miss increased 460%. In the U.S., drowsy drivers are responsible for a fifth of all motor vehicle accidents and some 8,000 deaths annually. It is estimated that 80,000 drivers fall asleep at the wheel every day, 10% of them run off the road, and every two minutes, one of them crashes. Countless innocent people are hurt. There's now a vehicular homicide law in New Jersey (and some pending in other states) that includes driving without sleep for more than 24 hours in its definition of recklessness. There's a man in Florida who's serving a 15-year prison term for vehicular homicide—he'd been awake for 30-some hours when he crashed his company's truck into a group of cars waiting for a light to change, killing three people. I would not want to be the CEO of the company bearing responsibility for those preventable deaths.

Sleep deprivation among employees poses other kinds of risks to companies as well. With too little sleep, people do things that no CEO in his or her right mind would allow. All over the world, people are running heavy and dangerous machinery or guarding secure sites and buildings while they're exhausted. Otherwise intelligent, well-mannered managers do all kinds of things they'd never do if they were rested—they may get angry at employees, make unsound decisions that affect the future of their companies, and give muddled presentations before their colleagues, customers, the press, or shareholders.

What should companies be doing to address the sleep problem?

People in executive positions should set behavioral expectations and develop corporate sleep policies, just as they already have concerning behaviors like smoking or sexual harassment. It's important to have a policy limiting scheduled work—ideally to no more than 12 hours a day, and exceptionally to no more than 16 consecutive hours. At least 11 consecutive hours of rest should be provided every 24 hours. Furthermore, employees should not be scheduled to work more than 60 hours a week and not be permitted to work more than 80 hours a week. When working at night or on extended shifts, employees should not be scheduled to work more than four or five consecutive days, and certainly no more than six consecutive days. People need at least one day off a week, and ideally two in a row, in order to avoid building up a sleep deficit.

Now, managers will often rationalize overscheduling employees. I hear them say that if their employees aren't working, they will be out partying and not sleeping anyway. That may be true for some irresponsible individuals, but it doesn't justify scheduling employees to work a hundred hours a week so that they can't possibly get an adequate amount of sleep. Of course, some circumstances may arise in which you need someone to remain at work for more than 16 consecutive hours. The night security guard, for example, can't just walk off the job if his replacement isn't there, so you will need to have a provision for exceptional circumstances, such as offering transportation home for a sleep-deprived worker.

Companies also need executive policies. For example, I would advise executives to avoid taking red-eye flights, which severely disrupt sleep. If someone must travel overnight internationally, the policy should allow the executive to take at least a day to adapt to the sleep deprivation associated with the flight and the new time zone before driving or conducting business. Such a policy requires some good schedule planning, but the time spent making the adjustments will be worth it, for the traveler will be more functional before going into that important meeting. And the sleep policy should not permit anyone, under any circumstances, to take an overnight flight and then drive to a business meeting somewhere—period. He or she should at least be provided a taxi, car service, or shuttle.

Companies can do other things to promote healthy sleep practices among employees. Educational programs about sleep, health, and safety should be mandatory. Employees should learn to set aside an adequate amount of time for sleep each night and to keep their bedrooms dark and quiet and free of all electronic devices—televisions, BlackBerries, and so on. They should learn about the ways alcohol and caffeine interfere with sleep. When someone is sleep deprived, drinking alcohol only makes things worse, further eroding performance and increasing the propensity to fall asleep while also interfering with the ability to stay asleep. Additionally, companies should provide annual screening for sleep disorders in order to identify those who might be at risk. For example, this past year our team launched a Web-based screening survey that any law enforcement officer in the U.S. can take to help identify whether he or she is suffering from sleep apnea, restless legs syndrome, narcolepsy, or other sleep disorders. Those whose answers place them at high risk are referred for evaluation and treatment by a specialist accredited by the American Academy of Sleep Medicine. (Accredited sleep centers may be found at www.sleepcenters.org.)

Finally, I would recommend that supervisors undergo training in sleep and fatigue management and that they promote good sleep behavior. People should learn to treat sleep as a serious matter. Both the company and the employees bear a shared responsibility to ensure that everyone comes to work well rested.

This corporate sleep policy of yours sounds a little draconian, if not impossible, given people's crazy schedules.

I don't think it's draconian at all. Business travelers expect that their pilots won't drink before flying an airplane, and all of us expect that no driver on the highway will have a blood alcohol level above the legal limit. Many executives already realize that the immediate effect of sleep loss on individuals and on overall corporate performance is just as important. A good sleep policy is smart business strategy. People think they're saving time and being more productive by not sleeping, but in fact they are cutting their productivity drastically. Someone who has adequate sleep doesn't nod off in an important meeting with a customer. She can pay attention to her task for longer periods of time and bring her whole intelligence and creativity to bear on the project at hand.

What do you think about the use of drugs that help people fall asleep or that shut off the urge to sleep?

These agents should be used only after a thorough evaluation of the causes of insomnia or excessive daytime sleepiness. Patients too often think there's a silver bullet for a problem like insomnia, and doctors too easily prescribe pills as part of a knee-jerk reaction to patient requests during the final minutes of an office visit. The causes of insomnia are subtle and need to be carefully investigated. These can be from too much caffeine, an irregular schedule, anxiety or depression, physical problems such as arthritis, use of other medications, and so on—and only a careful evaluation by a doctor experienced in sleep medicine can uncover the causes. I once saw a professor who complained of difficulty sleeping at night, and only after taking a careful history did we find that he was drinking 20 cups of coffee a day. He didn't even realize he was drinking that much and didn't think about the fact that so much caffeine, which has a six- to nine-hour half-life, would interfere with his ability to sleep. Prescribing a sleeping pill for his insomnia without identifying the underlying cause would have been a mistake.

There are non-pharmacological treatments for insomnia that seem very promising, by the way. Cognitive behavioral therapy, or CBT, helps people recognize and change thoughts and behaviors that might be keeping them awake at night. A researcher named Dr. Gregg Jacobs at Harvard Medical School has reported that CBT works better over both the short and the long term than sleeping pills do.

Sometimes executives simply have to function without much sleep. What are some strategies they can use to get by until they can go to bed?

Though there is no known substitute for sleep, there are a few strategies you can use to help sustain performance temporarily until you can get a good night's sleep. Obviously, executives can drink caffeine, which is the most widely used wake-promoting therapeutic in the world. Naps can be very effective at restoring performance, and if they are brief—less than a half hour—they will induce less grogginess upon awakening. Being in a novel or engaging circumstance will also help you stay alert. Exercise, standing in an upright position, and exposure to bright light are all very helpful. Human beings are amazingly sensitive to light. In fact, the color of light may also be important. Exposure to shorter wavelength blue light is particularly effective in suppressing melatonin production, thereby allowing us to stay awake during our biological night. Photon for photon, looking up at the blue sky, for example, is more effective in both resetting our biological clock and enhancing our alertness than looking down at the green grass.

While all these things can help an executive function in an emergency, I must reiterate that he or she should still not drive when sleep deprived, even if a cup of coffee or a walk on a sunny day seems to help for a little while.

Do you get enough sleep?

Like everyone else, I try to, but I don't always achieve it.

Notes

1. Dr. Czeisler is the incumbent of an endowed professorship donated to Harvard by Cephalon and consults for a number of companies, including Actelion, Cephalon, Coca-Cola, Hypnion, Pfizer, Respironics, Sanofi-Aventis, Takeda, and Vanda.

What's New in Sleep?

SLEEP SCIENCE IS ADVANCING on a number of frontiers that, over time, may cause us to rethink everything from our personal habits to public policy. Here's a short sampling of these new developments.

Sleep is power

Your mother was right—to perform at your best, you need sleep. Discoveries about sleep cycles have given researchers new insight into the specific roles sleep plays in overall health and performance. For example, there is growing evidence that sleep aids in immune function, memory consolidation, learning, and organ function. "Some researchers now think sleep may be the missing link when it comes to overall health, safety, and productivity," says Darrel Drobnich, the senior director of government and transportation affairs for the National Sleep Foundation. One new field of study is looking at a specific correlation between sleep and productivity, and the benefits of what sleep researchers call a "power nap"—a 20-minute period of sleep in the afternoon that heads off problems associated with cumulative sleep deficit.

Move over, Ambien

Ambien, the sleep aid from drugmaker Sanofi-Aventis, is now de rigueur for the sleepless, ringing up $1.4 billion annually in U.S. sales alone. While Ambien has fewer side effects than most over-the-counter sleep aids, it's still a blunt instrument, neurophysiologically speaking. "All of the current products on the market, including Ambien, take a sledgehammer to specific receptors in the brain," says Dr. Robert McCarley, the head of psychiatry at Boston VA Medical Center and a professor of psychiatry at Harvard Medical School. "They have several negative side effects, ranging from disassociated states of consciousness to potential addiction. They also tend to lose their effectiveness over time." Researchers hope a new family of sleep-inducing drugs will function closer to the body's natural sleep mechanisms and so avoid problems associated with sedatives like Ambien. One such new drug—Rozerem, from Japanese drug giant Takeda—targets melatonin receptors in the brain. As researchers learn more about the body's internal sleep mechanisms, McCarley believes, sleep aids will inevitably improve.

On the other side of the equation, the pharmaceutical company Cephalon is now marketing modafinil, a drug that helps people function well on very little sleep without suffering the ill effects of common stimulants. Sold under the commercial trade name Provigil in the U.S., modafinil was originally prescribed to treat narcolepsy; it's now used to promote wakefulness among those who can't afford to go to sleep (such as field soldiers in war zones). Studies have shown that subjects taking modafinil are able to stay alert with only eight hours of sleep during an 88-hour period. While modafinil sounds like a dream drug, no one yet knows what effects may result from more than occasional use.

Car drowse alarms

By the end of the decade, automakers will offer cars outfitted with devices designed to keep drowsy drivers from falling asleep at the wheel. Some may use cameras to scan drivers' eyes for droopiness, or to sense when people are loosening their grip on the steering wheel, and then sound an alarm. In 2005, Ford and Volvo announced that they were working on a system called Driver Alert, consisting of a camera that measures the distance between the vehicle and the markings on the surface of the road. If the driver starts to swerve, an alarm goes off and a text warning appears on the dashboard. Another approach under consideration by the U.S. National Highway Traffic Safety Administration is the development of "intelligent" highways equipped with specialized sensors that continuously track vehicle trajectory and speed.

Tomorrow's workforce needs sleep now

Businesses need an educated workforce; ironically, school is interfering. The current high school schedule in the U.S., which typically begins around 7:20 AM, threatens the neurological development and health of adolescents, whose homeostatic drive operates differently from adults'. Most teens experience a delayed sleep phase, in which melatonin is released around 11 PM–an hour later than in most adults. Students who finally go to sleep by midnight and wake at 6 experience a chronic sleep deficit, which disrupts their ability to learn and puts them and you at risk on the roads. In the U.S., researchers and sleep advocates are now working closely with school districts, communities, and educators to change school start times so that students can get more sleep.

—Bronwyn Fryer

Originally published in October 2006
Reprint R0610B

Decisions and Desire

GARDINER MORSE

Executive Summary

WHEN WE MAKE DECISIONS, we're not always in charge. One moment we hotheadedly let our emotions get the better of us; the next, we're paralyzed by uncertainty. Then we'll pull a brilliant decision out of thin air—and wonder how we did it. Though we may have no idea how decision making happens, neuroscientists peering deep into our brains are beginning to get the picture. What they're finding may not be what you want to hear, but it's worth listening.

We have dog brains, basically, with human cortexes stuck on top. By watching the brain in action as it deliberates and decides, neuroscientists are finding that not a second goes by that our animal brains aren't conferring with our modern cortexes to influence their choices. Scientists have discovered, for example, that the "reward" circuits in the brain that activate in response to cocaine, chocolate, sex, and music also find pleasure in the mere anticipation of making money—or getting revenge. And the "aversion" circuits that react to the threat of physical pain also respond with disgust when we feel cheated by a partner.

In this article, HBR senior editor Gardiner Morse describes the experiments that illuminate the aggressive participation of our emotion-driven animal brains in decision making. This research also shows that our emotional brains needn't always operate beneath our radar. While our dog brains sometimes hijack our higher cognitive functions to drive bad, or at least illogical, decisions, they play an important part in rational decision making as well. The more we understand about how we make decisions, the better we can manage them.

W HEN WE MAKE DECISIONS, we're not always in charge. We can be too impulsive or too deliberate for our own good; one moment we hotheadedly let our emotions get the better of us, and the next we're paralyzed by uncertainty. Then we'll pull a brilliant decision out of thin air—and wonder how we did it. Though we may have no idea how decision making happens, neuroscientists peering into our brains are beginning to get the picture. What they're finding may not be what you want to hear, but it's worth your while to listen.

The closer scientists look, the clearer it becomes how much we're like animals. We have dog brains, basically, with a human cortex stuck on top, a veneer of civilization. This cortex is an evolutionarily recent invention that plans, deliberates, and decides. But not a second goes by that our ancient dog brains aren't conferring with our modern cortexes to influence their choices—for better and for worse—and without us even knowing it.

Using scanning devices that measure the brain's activity, scientists can glimpse how the different parts of our brain, ancient and modern, collaborate and compete when we make decisions. Science is not going to produce anytime soon a formula for good decision making or for manipulating people's decisions (the hype surrounding "neuromarketing" notwithstanding). But the more we understand how we make decisions, the better we can manage them.

Into the Deep

Consider what happens beneath the brain's surface when people play the ultimatum game, a venerable economics experiment that pits participants against each other in a simple negotiation: One player has $10 to split with a second player—let's say you're the recipient. She can offer you any amount, from zero to $10, and she gets to keep the change—but only if you accept her offer. You are free to reject any offer, but if you do, neither of you gets anything. According to game theory, you should accept whatever she offers, however measly, because getting some money is better than getting none.

Of course, it doesn't work like that. In these experiments, when the offer dwindles to a few dollars, people on the receiving end consistently turn it down, forfeiting a free couple of bucks for—well, for what, exactly? Ask these participants and they'll tell you, in so many words, that they rejected the lowball offer because they were ticked off at the stingy partner (who, remember, loses her share, too). Not exactly a triumph of reason. This sounds like the dog brain at work, and it is.

Alan Sanfey, a cognitive neuroscientist at the University of Arizona, and colleagues used fMRI scans to look into people's brains while they played this game. (For a brief description of brain-scanning techniques, see the insert "Spots on Brains" at the end of this article.) As offers became increasingly unfair, the anterior insula, a part of the animal brain involved in negative emotions including anger and disgust, became more and more active, as if registering growing outrage. Meanwhile, part of the higher brain, an area of the prefrontal cortex involved in goal orientation (in this case, making money) was busy, too, assessing the situation. By tracking the activity of these two regions, Sanfey mapped what appeared to be a struggle between emotion and reason as each sought to influence the players' decisions. Punish the bastard? Or take the money, even though the deal stinks? When the disgusted anterior insula was more active than the rational goal-oriented prefrontal cortex—in a sense, when it was shouting louder—the players rejected the offer. When the prefrontal cortex dominated, the players took the money. (For a tour of the brain, see the insert "Three Brains in One" at the end of this article.)

Experiments like these illuminate the aggressive participation of our emotion-driven animal brains in all kinds of decision making. And they're beginning to expose the complex dance of primitive brain circuits involved in feelings of reward and aversion as we make choices. In the ultimatum game, it certainly looks as if our dog brains sometimes hijack our higher cognitive functions to drive bad or, at least, illogical decisions. But, as we shall see, our animal brains play an important part in rational decision making as well.

Emotion and Reason

Most of us are taught from early on that sound decisions come from a cool head, as the neurologist Antonio Damasio noted in his 1994 book *Descartes' Error.* The last thing one would want would be the intrusion of emotions in the methodical process of decision making. The high-reason view, Damasio writes, assumes that "formal logic will, by itself, get us to the best available solution for any problem. . . . To obtain the best results, emotions must be kept out." Damasio's research demolished that notion. Building on the work of many thinkers in the field, including Marsel Mesulam, Lennart Heimer, and Mortimer Mishkin, Damasio showed that patients with damage to the part of the prefrontal cortex that processes emotions (or, in a way, "listens" to them) often struggle with making even routine decisions.

A patient named Elliot was among the first to raise this weird possibility in Damasio's mind 20 years earlier. Elliot had been an exemplary husband, father, and businessman. But he began to suffer from severe headaches and lose track of work responsibilities. Soon, his doctors discovered an orange-sized brain tumor that was pushing into his frontal lobes, and they carefully removed it, along with some damaged brain tissue. It was during his recovery that family and friends discovered (as Damasio put it) that "Elliot was no longer Elliot." Though his language and intelligence were fully intact, at work he became distractible and couldn't manage his schedule. Faced with an organizational task, he'd deliberate for an entire afternoon about how to approach the problem. Should he organize the papers he was working on by date? The size of the document? Relevance to the case?

In effect, he was doing the organizational task too well, considering every possible option—but at the expense of achieving the larger goal. He could no longer effectively reach decisions, particularly personal and social ones, and despite being repeatedly shown this flaw, he could not correct it.

Though brain scans revealed isolated damage to the central (or ventromedial) portion of Elliot's frontal lobes, tests showed that his IQ, memory, learning, language, and other capacities were fine. But when Elliot was tested for emotional responses, the true nature of his deficit emerged. After viewing emotionally charged images—pictures of injured people and burning houses—Elliot revealed that things that had once evoked strong emotions no longer stirred him. He felt nothing.

Damasio and his colleagues have since studied over 50 patients with brain damage like Elliot's who share this combination of emotional and decision-making defects. And researchers have found that patients with injuries to parts of the limbic system, an ancient group of brain structures important in generating emotions, also struggle with making decisions. There's something critical to decision making in the conversation between emotion and reason in the brain, but what?

Call it gut. Or hunch. Or, more precisely, "prehunch," to use Damasio's term. In a famous series of experiments designed by Damasio's colleague Antoine Bechara at the University of Iowa, patients with Elliot's emotion-dampening type of brain damage were found to be unusually slow to detect a losing proposition in a card game. (Malcolm Gladwell offers an account of this game in his best seller *Blink*.)

In the game, players picked cards from red and blue decks, winning and losing play money with each pick.

The players were hooked up to lie-detector-like devices that measure skin conductance response, or SCR, which climbs as your stress increases and your palms sweat. Most players get a feeling that there's something amiss with the red decks after they turn over about 50 cards, and after 30 more cards, they can explain exactly what's wrong. But just ten cards into the game, their palms begin sweating when they reach for the red decks. Part of their brains *know* the red deck is a bad bet, and they begin to avoid it—even though they won't consciously recognize the problem for another 40 cards and won't be able to explain it until 30 cards after that. Long before they have a hunch about the red deck, a subconscious prehunch warns them away from it.

Though the brain-damaged patients eventually figured out that the red decks were rigged against them, they never developed palm-dampening SCRs. And, even though they consciously knew better, they continued to pick red cards. What were they missing? The injured parts of their brains in the prefrontal cortex seemed unable to process the emotional signals that guide decision making. Without this emotion interpreter pushing them in the right direction (toward the winning decks), these patients were left spinning their wheels, unable to act on what they knew. They couldn't decide, apparently, what was in their own best interest. You could say they lacked good judgment.

Risk and Reward

You don't have to be a neuroscientist to see how the emotional brain can badly distort judgment. Just ask any parent. From the toddler climbing the shelves to get candy to the teenager sneaking off for unprotected sex, kids have a dangerous shortage of common sense. Their bad behavior often looks consciously defiant (and sometimes it is), but the real problem may be that their brains haven't yet developed the circuitry that judiciously balances risks and rewards to yield levelheaded decisions. This is where the neuroscientists can offer special insight.

The brain's frontal lobes, so critical to decision making, don't fully mature until after puberty. Until then, the neuronal wiring that connects the prefrontal cortex to the rest of the brain is still under construction. Meanwhile, the parts of the brain that incite impulsive behavior seem particularly primed in teenagers. For instance, Gregory Berns and colleagues at Emory University found that certain still-developing circuits in adolescents' brains become hyperactive when the kids experience pleasurable novel stimuli. An adolescent's brain is wired to favor immediate and surprising rewards, even when the teen knows full well that pursuing them may be a bad idea.

In a sense, teenagers have yet to complete the wiring that manifests as willpower. The prefrontal cortex, it appears, is the seat of willpower—the ability to take the long-term perspective in evaluating risks and rewards. As such, this area of the brain is in close contact with the structures and circuits of the emotional animal brain that seek gratification and alert us to danger.

Much of the traffic between the primitive and modern parts of our brains is devoted to this conscious calculation of risks and rewards. Though animals' reward and aversion circuitry is a lot like ours, unlike most animals, we can look out at the horizon and contemplate what might flow from a decision to chase immediate gratification. And we can get immediate pleasure from the prospect of some future gratification.

Thrill of the Hunt

Jean-Paul Sartre was a famous womanizer, but for him the excitement was in the chase. As Louis Menand wrote of him in the *New Yorker,* "He took enormous satisfaction in the conquest but little pleasure in the sex (and so he usually terminated the physical part of his affairs coldly and quickly)." Sartre's pursuits underscore a fundamental fact about how our brains experience rewards. Whether it's reacting to a sexual conquest, a risky business deal, or an addictive drug, the brain often distinguishes clearly between the thrill of the hunt and the pleasure of the feast.

The brain's desire for rewards is a principal source of bad judgment, in teenagers and adults alike. But it would be wrong to assign blame for ill-advised reward seeking to a single part of the brain. Rather, the brain has a complex reward system of circuits that spans from bottom to top, old to new. These circuits interact to motivate us to search for things we like and to let us know when we've found them. Hans Breiter, a neuroscientist at Massachusetts General Hospital, was among the first to use fMRI to explore this reward system. In collaboration with the behavioral economist Daniel Kahneman and colleagues, Breiter showed that the brain regions that respond to cocaine or morphine are the same ones that react to the prospect of getting money and to actually receiving it. It's perhaps no surprise that chocolate, sex, music, attractive faces, and sports cars also arouse this reward system. Curiously, revenge does too, as we shall see. (Though Breiter's work suggests there's great overlap between the brain's reward-seeking and loss-aversion circuits, for simplicity this article will discuss them separately.)

The reward circuits depend on a soup of chemicals to communicate, chief among them the neurotransmitter dopamine. Dopamine is often referred to as the brain's "pleasure chemical," but that's a misnomer. It's more of a pleasure facilitator or regulator. (The writer Steven Johnson calls it a "pleasure accountant.") Produced in the ancient structures of our animal brains, it helps to regulate the brain's appetite for rewards and its sense of how well rewards meet expectations.

Well-regulated appetites are crucial to survival. Without these drives, our ancestors wouldn't have hunted for food or pursued sexual partners, and you wouldn't be here to read this article. By the same token, unchecked reward seeking isn't very adaptive either, as patients with disrupted dopamine systems demonstrate. Consider what happened to Bruce (as I will call him), a computer programmer, who had had no history of psychiatric problems. Bruce had never been a gambler, but at the age of 41, he abruptly began compulsively gambling, frittering away thousands of dollars in a matter of weeks over the Internet. He began to shop compulsively, too, buying things that he neither needed nor wanted. And to his wife's growing alarm, he began to demand sex several times a day.

Bruce's story would be little more than a footnote in the medical literature but for one twist: He had Parkinson's disease, and just before his compulsions began, his neurologist had added a new drug to his regimen—pramipexole—which relieves the tremors of the disease by mimicking dopamine. When Bruce described his worrisome new passions to his neurologist, the doctor, suspecting the pramipexole might be involved, advised him to reduce his dose. Bruce stopped taking the drug altogether, and two days later, his desires—to gamble, to shop, to have sex many times a day—simply vanished. It was, he said, "like a light switch being turned off."

Cases like Bruce's reveal the extraordinary power of our dopamine-fueled appetite for rewards—as distinct from the rewards themselves—to ride roughshod over reason. But what about the rest of us who go about our reward-seeking business in apparently more balanced ways? We clearly do a better job of weighing trade-offs than Bruce did, but much of the same circuitry is at work—and, as such, sometimes our pursuits aren't as rational as we think they are.

SHOW ME THE MONEY

Economists have assumed that people work because they place value on the things money can buy (or, in economic terms, they gauge "utility"). But neuroscience studies show how chasing money is its own reward. In one set of experiments, Stanford neuroscientist Brian Knutson used fMRI to watch subjects' brains as they reacted to the prospect of receiving money. Among the brain regions that lit up in this experiment was the nucleus accumbens, signaling in its primitive way, "You *want* this." (Rats with electrodes planted near the accumbens will press a lever to stimulate the area until they drop from exhaustion.) The higher the potential monetary reward, the more active the accumbens became. But activity ceased by the time the subjects actually *received* the money—suggesting that it was the anticipation, and not the reward itself, that aroused them.

As Knutson puts it, the nucleus accumbens seems to act as a gas pedal that accelerates our drive for rewards, while the relevant part of the prefrontal cortex is the steering wheel that directs reward seeking toward specific goals. When it comes to making money, having the accumbens on the gas pedal is often desirable—it motivates high performance at work among other things. But when you step on the gas, you want to be pointed in the right direction.

SWEET REVENGE

It's no surprise that the prospect of money or food or sex stimulates our reward circuits. But revenge? Consider Clara Harris. Her name may not ring a bell, but her case probably will. Harris is the Houston dentist who, upon encountering her husband and his receptionist-turned-mistress in a hotel parking lot in 2002, ran him down with her Mercedes. What was she *thinking?* According to an Associated Press report at the time of her murder conviction in 2003, Harris testified, "I didn't know who was driving . . . everything seemed like a dream." As she put it, "I wasn't thinking anything."

No one can know exactly what was going on in Harris's mind when she hit the accelerator. But her own testimony and the jury's conclusion that she acted with "sudden passion" suggest a woman in a vengeful rage whose emotional brain overwhelmed any rational deliberation. We do know that a desire to retaliate, to punish others' bad behavior, however mild, even at personal cost, can skew decision making. Recall the ultimatum card game, in which a player could accept or reject another player's offer of money. Alan Sanfey's brain scans of people feeling vengeful in these games show how (at least in part) a sense of moral disgust manifests in the brain. But anyone who has settled a score knows that a desire for vengeance is more than an angry response to a bad feeling. Revenge, as they say, is sweet— even *contemplating* it is.

When University of Zurich researchers Dominique
J. F. de Quervain, Ernst Fehr, and colleagues scanned
subjects with a PET device during an ultimatum-like
game, they found certain reward circuits in the brain's
striatum activated when players anticipated, and then
actually punished, ill-behaved partners. What's more, the
greater the activation of the striatum, the greater the
subjects' willingness to incur costs for the opportunity to
deliver punishment. At the same time, the researchers
saw activation in the medial prefrontal cortex, the deliberative part of the higher brain that's thought to weigh
risks and rewards. Once again, neuroscientists seem to
have caught on camera an engagement between the
emotional and reasoning parts of the brain.

These same brain regions—the reward-seeking striatum and the deliberative prefrontal cortex, both of which
are activated by the pleasing possibility of revenge—also
light up when people anticipate giving rewards to partners who cooperate. Though the players' behaviors are
opposite—bestowing a reward versus exacting punishment—their brains react in the same way in eager anticipation of a satisfying social experience.

Fear and Loathing

Like the brain's reward circuits, its systems for sensing
and making decisions about risks are powerful and
prone to error. Often this fact confronts us directly.
Many people, for instance, have a paralyzing fear of flying that's unrelated to its true risks. All the time, people
make the irrational decision to travel by car rather than
fly, believing on a gut level that it's safer, even though
they know it's not.

This behavior is partly the work of the amygdala, a
structure near the base of the brain. Colin Camerer, a

behavioral and experimental economist at the California
Institute of Technology, calls the amygdala an "internal
hypochondriac," which provides quick and dirty emotional signals in response to potential threats. It's also
been called the "fear site," responsible for both produc-
ing fear responses and learning from experience to be
afraid of certain stimuli. The amygdala responds instan-
taneously to all manner of perceived potential threats
and pays particular attention to social cues. This leads to
good and, often, very bad decisions.

FACE YOUR FEAR

Look at how the amygdala influences first impressions:
Brain-scanning experiments show that it activates when
people see spiders, snakes, frightening expressions, faces
that look untrustworthy—and faces of another race. It's
easy to see how a *"that's a threat"* response to a snake
could guide good decisions, particularly a million years
ago out on the savanna. But a gut reaction that says
"watch out" when you see a face of a different race?

MRI studies have shown that the amygdala becomes
more active when whites see black faces than when they
see white faces; similarly, in blacks, the amygdala reacts
more to white faces than black ones. Taken alone, this
finding says nothing about people's conscious attitudes.
But research by Harvard social ethicist Mahzarin Banaji
and colleagues shows that even people who consciously
believe they have no racial bias often do have negative
unconscious feelings toward "outgroups"—people not
like themselves. (For more on this work, see "How
(Un)ethical Are You?" by Banaji, Max Bazerman, and
Dolly Chugh in the December 2003 issue of *Harvard
Business Review*.) Investigators have found, too, that the

greater a person's unconscious bias on these tests, the more active the amygdala.

Researchers are very cautious in interpreting these findings. The facile conclusion that our animal brains automatically fear people of other races is probably not right. But this and related work does suggest that our brains are wired so that we're primed in a way—we learn easily—to go on alert when we encounter people who seem different. (Research also suggests that this primed response can be reduced by positive exposure to people of other races—but that's a different article.)

On the one hand, we should be happy that our amygdalas warn us of potential dangers before our conscious brains grasp that something's amiss. But a brain circuit that was indispensable to our ancestors, warning them away from legitimate threats like snakes, certainly contributes to an array of bad and irrational decisions today. In the case of our readiness to fear outgroups, think of the countless missed opportunities and just plain bad decisions made by good people who consciously hold no racial biases but who nonetheless have gone with an inchoate gut sense to withhold a job offer, deny a promotion, or refuse a loan because their amygdalas, for no good reason, said, "Watch out."

WHEEL OF MISFORTUNE

The amygdala's role in warning us about perils real and imagined seems to extend even to the threat of losing money. In Breiter's lab, researchers monitored brain activity while volunteers watched images of roulette-like wheels, each with a spinning arrow that would come to a stop on a particular dollar amount, either a gain, a loss, or zero. It was obvious at a glance that some wheels were likely to produce dollar wins while others were clearly losers. When the losing wheels spun, subjects' amygdalas activated even before the arrows stopped, signaling their discomfort about the losses they saw coming.

Beyond the amygdala, the brain has another risk-aversion region that steers us from disagreeable stimuli. Recall in the ultimatum game that it was the anterior insula that reacted with disgust to the other player's rotten offer; this region also activates when people think they're about to experience pain or see something shocking. Like our reward-seeking circuitry, loss-avoidance circuits involving the amygdala and anterior insula serve us well—when they're not driving us to overact and make bad decisions.

Consider investment decisions. Investors who should be focused on maximizing utility routinely take risks when they shouldn't and don't take risks when they should. (Among the biases that skew utility seeking is that people weigh equivalent losses and gains differently; that is, they feel better about avoiding a $100 loss than securing a $100 gain.) To see what's going on in their heads when people make bad investment choices, Stanford researchers Camelia Kuhnen and Brian Knutson had volunteers play an investment game while their brains were scanned with fMRI.

In the game, volunteers chose among two different stocks and a bond, adjusting their picks with each round of the game based on the investments' performance in the previous round. While the bond returned a constant amount, one stock was more likely to make money over a series of trades (the "good" stock) and the other to lose money (the "bad" stock). Kuhnen and Knutson found that, even when players had developed a sense of which was the good stock, they'd still often head for the riskless bond after they'd made a losing stock choice—what the researchers called a risk-aversion mistake. In other words, even though they should have known to pick the good stock on each round, when they got stung with a loss they'd often irrationally retreat.

The MRI scans revealed this risk-aversiveness unfolding. Prior to choosing the safety of the bond, the players' anterior insulas would activate, signaling their (perhaps not-yet-conscious) anxiety. In fact, the more active this primitive risk-anticipating brain region, the more risk averse players were—often to their own detriment.

Know Your Brain

Controversial though some of his ideas may be, Freud wasn't so far off when he posited the struggle between the animalistic id and the rational superego. But he may have been too generous in his assessment of the superego's ability to channel our emotions. Neuroscientists are showing that the emotional and deliberative circuits in the brain are in constant interaction (some would say struggle), and the former, for better or for worse, often holds sway. What's more, with each new study it becomes clearer just how quickly, subtly, and powerfully our unconscious impulses work. Flash a picture of an angry or a happy face on a screen for a few hundredths of a second, and your amygdala instantly reacts—but *you*, your conscious self, have no idea what you saw.

MGH's Breiter believes the more we learn about the brain science of motivation, the more readily it can be applied in business. "People's decision-making and management styles probably arise from common motivational impulses in the brain," he points out. "If a manager is hardwired to be more risk seeking, or risk avoiding, or more driven to pursue a goal than to achieve it, that's going to affect how he manages and makes decisions." With our increasingly clear understanding of how basic motivations affect conscious decisions, Breiter says, it should be possible to tailor incentives accordingly. A manager who shows a preference for the hunt might, for instance, be well served by incentives that increase his motivation to reach goals rather than simply chase them.

Neuroscience research also teaches us that our emotional brains needn't always operate beneath our radar. Richard Peterson, a psychiatrist who applies behavioral economics theory in his investment consulting business, advises clients to cultivate emotional self-awareness, notice their moods as they happen, and reflect on how their moods may influence their decisions. In particular, he advises people to pay close attention to feelings of excitement (a heightened expression of reward seeking) and fear (an intense expression of loss aversion) and ask, when such a feeling arises, "What causes this? Where did these feelings come from? What is the context in which I'm having these feelings?" By consciously monitoring moods and the related decisions, Peterson says, people can become more savvy users of their gut feelings.

This advice may sound familiar; it lies at the heart of books like *Blink* and Gary Klein's *The Power of Intuition,* which promise to help readers harness their gut feelings. But for executives taught to methodically frame problems, consider alternatives, collect data, weigh the options, and then decide, cultivating emotional self-awareness may seem like a dispensable exercise—or at least not a critical tool in decision making. The picture emerging from the neuroscience labs is that you ignore your gut at your own peril. Whether you're negotiating an acquisition, hiring an employee, jockeying for a promotion, granting a loan, trusting a partner—taking any gamble—be aware that your dog brain is busy in increasingly predictable, measurable ways with its own assessment of the situation and often its own agenda. You'd better be paying attention.

Spots on Brains

EYE-POPPING COLOR IMAGES of brain scans in the popular press imply that scientists are pinpointing the precise location in the brain of feelings like fear, disgust, pleasure, and trust. But the researchers doing this work are highly circumspect about just what these colorful spots show. The two most common scanning methods, PET (positron emission tomography) and fMRI (functional magnetic resonance imaging), offer only approximations of what's really going on in the brain. PET, the older and less popular of the two, measures blood flow in the brain; fMRI measures the amount of oxygen in the blood. Local blood flow and oxygenation indicate how active a part of the brain is but offer a crude snapshot at best. These scanners typically can't see anything smaller than a peppercorn and can take only one picture every two seconds. But neural activity in the brain can occur in a fraction of the space and time that scanners can reveal. Thus, the splashy images we see are impressionistic, and the conclusions researchers draw about them are usually qualified—and often disputed. Like the images themselves, the details of brain function are just beginning to come into focus.

Three Brains in One

THINK OF YOUR BRAIN as composed of three layers, the evolutionarily oldest and simplest at the center and the most modern and complex on the outside. At the top of the spinal cord—the center of the brain—lie the most primitive structures, ones we share with reptiles and fish, which control basic survival functions like breathing and hunger. Wrapped around these is the ancient limbic system, which we share with dogs and other mammals. Containing the thalamus, amygdala, and hippocampus, it is the seat of basic emotions such as fear, aggressiveness, and contentment. It's the part of the brain that allows your dog to seem so pleased that you're home while your fish couldn't care less.

Encasing these older structures is the modern cortex, the folded gray matter that we all recognize as the human brain. Dogs, chimps, and other mammals have cortexes, but ours has grown to a huge size. The cortex manages all sorts of higher brain processes like hearing and vision. The frontal lobes and, in particular, the prefrontal cortex (at the front of the frontal lobes) are the parts that make us human. They are the center of personality, reasoning, and abstract thought. Often, the prefrontal cortex is called the "executive" part of the brain because it considers input from throughout the brain in goal formation and planning.

Originally published in January 2006
Reprint R0601C

Leading by Feel

DAVID GERGEN, DANIEL GOLEMAN,
RONALD HEIFETZ, AND OTHERS

Executive Summary

LIKE IT OR NOT, leaders need to manage the mood of
their organizations. The most gifted leaders accomplish
that by using a mysterious blend of psychological abilities known as emotional intelligence. They are self-aware
and empathetic. They can read and regulate their own
emotions while intuitively grasping how others feel and
gauging their organization's emotional state.

But where does emotional intelligence come from,
and how do leaders learn to use it? In this article, 18
leaders and scholars (including business executives,
leadership researchers, psychologists, an autism expert,
and a symphony conductor) explore the nature and management of emotional intelligence—its sources, uses, and
abuses. Their responses varied, but some common
themes emerged: the importance of consciously—and
conscientiously—honing one's skills, the double-edged

nature of self-awareness, and the danger of letting any one emotional intelligence skill dominate. Among their observations:

Psychology professor John Mayer, who codeveloped the concept of emotional intelligence, warns managers not to be confused by popular definitions of the term, which suggest that if you have a certain set of personality traits then you automatically possess emotional intelligence. Neuropsychologist Elkhonon Goldberg agrees with professors Daniel Goleman and Robert Goffee that emotional intelligence can be learned—but only by people who already show an aptitude for it. Cult expert Janja Lalich points out that leaders can use their emotional intelligence skills for ill in the same way they can for good. "Sometimes the only difference is [the leader's] intent," she says. And business leaders Carol Bartz, William George, Sidney Harman, and Andrea Jung (of Autodesk, Medtronic, Harman International, and Avon respectively) describe situations in which emotional intelligence traits such as self-awareness and empathy have helped them and their companies perform at a higher level.

LIKE IT OR NOT, leaders need to manage the mood of their organizations. The most gifted leaders accomplish that by using a mysterious blend of psychological abilities known as emotional intelligence. They're self-aware and empathetic. They can read and regulate their own emotions while intuitively grasping how others feel and gauging their organization's emotional state.

But where does emotional intelligence come from? And how do leaders learn to use it? The management literature (and even common sense) suggests that both nature and nurture feed emotional intelligence. Part genetic predisposition, part life experience, and part old-fashioned training, emotional intelligence emerges in varying degrees from one leader to the next, and managers apply it with varying skill. Wisely and compassionately deployed, emotional intelligence spurs leaders, their people, and their organizations to superior performance; naively or maliciously applied, it can paralyze leaders or allow them to manipulate followers for personal gain.

We invited 18 leaders and scholars (including business executives, leadership researchers, psychologists, a neurologist, a cult expert, and a symphony conductor) to explore the nature and management of emotional intelligence—its sources, uses, and abuses. Their responses differed dramatically, but there were some common themes: the importance of consciously—and conscientiously—honing one's skills, the double-edged nature of self-awareness, and the danger of letting any one emotional intelligence skill dominate.

Be Realistic

John D. Mayer (jack.mayer@unh.edu) is a professor of psychology at the University of New Hampshire. He and Yale psychology professor Peter Salovey are credited with first defining the concept of emotional intelligence in the early 1990s.

THIS IS A TIME OF GROWING REALISM about emotional intelligence—especially concerning what it is and what it isn't. The books and articles that have helped popularize the concept have defined it as a loose collection of personality traits, such as self-awareness, optimism, and tolerance. These popular definitions have been accompanied by exaggerated claims about the importance of emotional intelligence. But diverse personality traits, however admirable, don't necessarily add up to a single definition of emotional intelligence. In fact, such traits are difficult to collectively evaluate in a way that reveals their relationship to success in business and in life.

Even when they're viewed in isolation, the characteristics commonly associated with emotional intelligence and success may be more complicated than they seem. For example, the scientific jury is out on how important self-awareness is to successful leadership. In fact, too much self-awareness can reduce self-esteem, which is often a crucial component of great leadership.

From a scientific (rather than a popular) standpoint, emotional intelligence is the ability to accurately perceive your own and others' emotions; to understand the signals that emotions send about relationships; and to manage your own and others' emotions. It doesn't necessarily include the qualities (like optimism, initiative, and self-confidence) that some popular definitions ascribe to it.

Researchers have used performance tests to measure people's accuracy at identifying and understanding emotions—for example, asking them to identify the emotions conveyed by a face or which among several situations is most likely to bring about happiness. People who get high scores on these tests are indeed different from others. In the business world, they appear better able to deal with customers' complaints or to mediate disputes, and they may excel at making strong and positive personal connections with subordinates and customers over the long term. Of course, emotional intelligence isn't the only way to attain success as a leader: A brilliant strategist who can maximize profits may be able to hire and keep talented employees even if he or she doesn't have strong personal connections with them.

Is there value in scales that, based on popular conceptions, measure qualities like optimism and self-confidence but label them emotional intelligence? Certainly these personality traits are important in business, so measuring and (sometimes) enhancing them can be useful. But recent research makes it clear that these characteristics are distinct from emotional intelligence as it is scientifically defined. A person high in emotional intelligence may be realistic rather than optimistic and insecure rather than confident. Conversely, a person may be highly self-confident and optimistic but lack emotional intelligence. The danger lies in assuming that because a person is optimistic or confident, he or she is also emotionally intelligent, when, in fact, the presence of those traits will tell you nothing of the sort.

Never Stop Learning

Daniel Goleman is the cochair of the Consortium for Research on Emotional Intelligence in Organizations based at Rutgers University's Graduate School of Applied and Professional Psychology in Piscataway, New Jersey.

YOU CAN BE A SUCCESSFUL LEADER without much emotional intelligence if you're extremely lucky and you've got everything else going for you: booming markets, bumbling competitors, and clueless higher-ups. If you're incredibly smart, you can cover for an absence of emotional intelligence until things get tough for the business. But at that point, you won't have built up the social capital needed to pull the best out of people under tremendous pressure. The art of sustained leadership is getting others to produce superior work, and high IQ alone is insufficient to that task.

The good news is that emotional intelligence can be learned and improved at any age. In fact, data show that, on average, people's emotional intelligence tends to increase as they age. But the specific leadership competencies that are based on emotional intelligence don't necessarily come through life experience. For example, one of the most common complaints I hear about leaders, particularly newly promoted ones, is that they lack empathy. The problem is that they were promoted because they were outstanding individual performers, and being a solo achiever doesn't teach you the skills necessary to understand other people's concerns.

Leaders who are motivated to improve their emotional intelligence can do so if they're given the right information, guidance, and support. The information they need is a candid assessment of their strengths and limitations from people who know them well and whose opinions they trust. The guidance they need is a specific developmental plan that uses naturally occurring workplace encounters as the laboratory for learning. The support they need is someone to talk to as they practice how to handle different situations, what to do when they've blown it, and how to learn from those setbacks. If leaders cultivate these resources and practice continually, they can develop specific emotional intelligence skills—skills that will last for years.

Watch the Language

Colleen Barrett is the president and corporate secretary of Dallas-based Southwest Airlines.

I've ALWAYS FELT that my intuition was pretty darn good, and I think I can read people well. I rely a ton on my gut. I know the mood of our different work groups. I know the expectations of our employees. I think people are generally born with a predisposition for this type of emotional awareness. But I certainly believe you can enhance your ability just from experience and learning. I've probably gotten better at it over the years because I read and listen to everything, and I'm constantly observing. I watch body language and how people interact.

The other day, I was talking to one of our officers, and he said, "How do you do that?" and I said, "How do I do what?" He was referring to a meeting we'd both been at earlier. I'd asked one of the presenters at the meeting, a fellow who reported to this officer, if he was feeling OK. The officer thought the employee was fine, but, it turns out, the poor guy had had a pretty traumatic experience in his personal life the night before. His presentation went well, but he seemed off to me, distracted. I suppose in order to have seen that, I must have been fairly attuned to what this fellow's presentations were usually like.

I often communicate on a passionate, emotional level—which can be a detriment, particularly for a woman in a predominantly male leadership group, as ours was for many years. There were times when I'd launch in on an issue and make gut-level assertions like, "Our customers feel this," and "Our employees feel that." Though everyone in the group would probably deny it,

I know that part of their reaction to my outbursts was, "Oh, that's just Colleen, and she's on a tangent," and they would tend to disregard what I was saying. I've learned to rely on calmer people around me to give me those raised eyebrows that say, "Lower the passion a little bit, and people will listen more." When I'm making my arguments, I have to really prepare and try to be—and this is very difficult for me—factual and dispassionate.

Build Pathways

***Steven Gutstein** (gutstein@connectionscenter.com) is a psychologist, autism expert, and codirector of Connections Center for Family and Personal Development in Houston.*

I WORK WITH AUTISTIC CHILDREN, a population typically defined by its lack of emotional intelligence. People with autism can't connect—indeed, they aren't really interested in connecting emotionally with others. Traditionally, the therapeutic approach with these kids has been to teach them to fake it. They are urged to make eye contact with others, to repress whatever distracting behaviors they may have, and to use social scripts. Many of these therapies have the appearance of being successful. People with autism do learn the scripts, and some even blend in.

The problem is, faking it never ceases to be work. So as autistic children become adults, they stop putting on the show. Among adults with Asperger's syndrome (a form of autism marked by average or above-average IQ), fewer than 12% hold jobs. Only 3% leave home. These findings make the case profoundly that one gets only so far on IQ. People need to connect emotionally, and with flexibility, in order to succeed. These findings also demonstrate that traditional therapies have not been successful at improving quality of life for autistic people.

My approach to teaching emotional intelligence skills to children with autism, which I call "relationship development intervention" (RDI), takes a different tack. It begins with a belief that people with autism can be taught to value relationships, to seek out interactions that are not merely transactional ("I will deal with you because there is something I want from you") but where the whole point is to enjoy the shared experience. Nonautistic people begin to have these kinds of relationships early in life; at about ten months, most babies start developing the capacity for social referencing, the appreciation that *my* actions should take into account *your* emotions. We now know from neuroimaging that at this stage some critical neural pathways are being laid down among all the structures in the limbic system, which regulates emotion and motivation. Autistic children typically don't develop those pathways.

But with RDI, which uses cognitive exercises and activities to motivate the children to learn specific behaviors rather than social scripts, I think we can create the neurological traffic to establish those pathways. Mind you, we are not curing autism. But we are teaching emotional intelligence. If people with autism can learn emotional intelligence, anyone can.

Get Motivated

Richard Boyatzis (reb2@cwru.edu) is a professor and the chair of the department of organizational behavior at

Case Western Reserve University's Weatherhead School of Management in Cleveland.

People can develop their emotional intelligence if they really want to. But many managers jump to the conclusion that their complement of emotional intelligence is predetermined. They think, "I could never be good at this, so why bother?" The central issue isn't a lack of ability to change; it's the lack of motivation to change.

Leadership development is not all that different from other areas in which people are trying to change their behaviors. Just look at the treatments for alcoholism, drug addiction, and weight loss: They all require the desire to change. More subtly, they all require a positive, rather than a negative, motivation. You have to want to change. If you think you'll lose your job because you're not adequately tuned in to your employees, you might become determinedly empathetic or compassionate for a time. But change driven by fear or avoidance probably isn't going to last. Change driven by hopes and aspirations, that's pursued because it's desired, will be more enduring.

There's no such thing as having too much emotional intelligence. But there is a danger in being preoccupied with, or overusing, one aspect of it. For example, if you overemphasize the emotional intelligence competencies of initiative or achievement, you'll always be changing things at your company. Nobody would know what you were going to do next, which would be quite destabilizing for the organization. If you overuse empathy, you might never fire anybody. If you overuse teamwork, you might never build diversity or listen to a lone voice. Balance is essential.

Train the Gifted

Elkhonon Goldberg (egneurocog@aol.com) is a clinical professor of neurology at New York University School of Medicine and the director of the Institute of Neuropsychology and Cognitive Performance in New York.

IN THE PAST, neuropsychologists were mostly concerned with cognitive impairment. Today, they are increasingly interested in the biological underpinnings of cognitive differences in people without impairments—including differences in people's emotional intelligence.

Emotional intelligence can be learned, to a degree. It's like mathematical or musical ability. Can you become a musician if you lack natural aptitude? Yes, you can, if you take lessons and practice enough. But will you ever be a Mozart? Probably not. In the same way, emotional intelligence develops through a combination of biological endowment and training. And people who don't have that endowment probably won't become deeply emotionally intelligent just through training. Trying to drum emotional intelligence into someone with no aptitude for it is an exercise in futility. I believe the best way to get emotionally intelligent leaders is to select for people who already show the basic qualities you want. Think about it: That's how athletic coaches operate. They don't just work with anyone who wants to play a sport; they train the naturally gifted. Business managers should do the same.

How do you identify the naturally gifted? I'd say you have to look for those with a genuine, instinctive interest in other people's experiences and mental worlds. It's an absolute prerequisite for developing emotional intelligence. If a manager lacks this interest, maybe your training resources are better directed elsewhere.

Seek Frank Feedback

Andrea Jung is the chair and CEO of Avon Products, which is based in New York.

EMOTIONAL INTELLIGENCE IS IN OUR DNA here at Avon because relationships are critical at every stage of our business. It starts with the relationships our 4.5 million independent sales reps have with their customers and goes right up through senior management to my office. So the emphasis on emotional intelligence is much greater here than it was at other companies in which I've worked. We incorporate emotional intelligence education into our development training for senior managers, and we factor in emotional intelligence competencies when we evaluate employees' performance.

Of all a leader's competencies, emotional and otherwise, self-awareness is the most important. Without it, you can't identify the impact you have on others. Self-awareness is very important for me as CEO. At my level, few people are willing to tell me the things that are hardest to hear. We have a CEO advisory counsel—ten people chosen each year from Avon offices throughout the world—and they tell me the good, the bad, and the ugly about the company. Anything can be said. It helps keep me connected to what people really think and how my actions affect them. I also rely on my children for honest appraisals. You can get a huge dose of reality by seeing yourself through your children's eyes, noticing the ways they react to and reflect what you say and do. My kids are part of my 360-degree feedback. They're the most honest of all.

I grew up in a very traditional Chinese family. My parents were concerned that the way I'd been raised—submissive, caring, and averse to conflict—would hinder my ability to succeed in the *Fortune* 500 environment. They were afraid I couldn't make the tough decisions. But I've learned how to be empathetic and still make hard decisions that are right for the company. These are not incompatible abilities. When Avon has had to close plants, for example, I've tried to act with compassion for the people involved. And I've gotten letters from some of the associates who were affected, expressing sadness but also saying thanks for the fair treatment. Leaders' use of emotional intelligence when making tough decisions is important to their success—and to the success of their organizations.

Gauge Your Awareness

Howard Book (hbwork@netsurf.net) is an associate professor in the department of psychiatry at the University of Toronto and an organizational consultant.

SELF-AWARENESS IS THE KEY emotional intelligence skill behind good leadership. It's often thought of as the ability to know how you're feeling and why, and the impact your feelings have on your behavior. But it also involves a capacity to monitor and control those strong but subliminal biases that all of us harbor and that can skew our decision making.

Consider, for example, a vice president who complained to me recently about his new hire, the head of sales. He found her to be unassertive, indecisive, unsure—hardly leadership material. When I talked to her, however, it turned out she felt her boss was sabotaging her career. The vice president had been hired only five months before she had, and he was oblivious to how his anxiety to please the CEO was causing him to micromanage. In doing so, the VP was undercutting the sales director's independence and confidence. His lack of self-awareness directly impaired her performance.

Experience and literature on the subject suggest that while both nature and nurture influence emotional intelligence, nurture is the more important factor. Indeed, this emphasis on environment is one of the hallmarks that differentiates emotional intelligence from cognitive intelligence, or IQ. Whereas cognitive intelligence is fixed by about the age of ten, emotional intelligence increases with age. So you can actually learn emotional intelligence skills like self-awareness. One simple way to measure your self-awareness is to ask a trusted friend or colleague to draw up a list of your strengths and weaknesses while you do the same. It can be an uncomfortable exercise, but the bigger the gap between your list and your helper's, the more work you probably have to do.

Sniff Out Signals

Robert Goffee (rgoffee@london.edu) is a professor of organizational behavior at London Business School and a cofounder of Creative Management Associates, an organizational consulting firm in London.

You NEED SOME DEGREE of emotional intelligence to be an effective leader, but you do see some one-hit wonders out there—people who have limited emo-

tional intelligence but can still excite a particular group.
The problem is, they can't transfer their success to
another organization. They got lucky and landed in a situation in which their passions happened to connect with
the organization's passions, but they probably wouldn't
be able to replicate that at another company. By contrast, true leaders can connect with different groups of
people in a variety of contexts.

To some extent, these one-hit wonders can learn how
to be emotionally intelligent. One component of emotional intelligence is "situation sensing"—the ability to
sniff out the signals in an environment and figure out
what's going on without being told. You can develop this
skill through jobs in which you're exposed to a wide
range of people and have a motive for watching their
reactions. For instance, Roche CEO Franz Humer is
highly skilled at detecting subtle cues and underlying
shifts of opinion. Humer told me and my colleague
Gareth Jones that he developed the skill while working as
a tour guide in his mid-twenties. Because he relied solely
on tips for his pay, Humer quickly learned how to size up
a group of as many as 100 people and figure out who was
likely to give him a tip. That way, he'd know where to
focus his attention. (For more on this example, see
"Why Should Anyone Be Led By You?" HBR September–
October 2000.)

I'd caution against overemphasizing any one aspect
of emotional intelligence; if these skills are developed
disproportionately, they can interfere with your relationships. If you're extremely self-aware but short on
empathy, you might come off as self-obsessed. If you're
excessively empathetic, you risk being too hard to read.
If you're great at self-management but not very trans-
parent, you might seem inauthentic. Finally, at times
leaders have to deliberately avoid getting too close to

the troops in order to ensure that they're seeing the bigger picture. Emotionally intelligent leaders know when to rein it in.

Engage Your Demons

David Gergen directs the Center for Public Leadership at Harvard University's John F. Kennedy School of Govern-ment in Cambridge, Massachusetts. He served as an adviser to presidents Nixon, Ford, Reagan, and Clinton.

AMERICAN HISTORY SUGGESTS not only that emotional intelligence is an indispensable ingredient of political leadership but also that it can be enhanced through sustained effort. George Washington had to work hard to control his fiery temper before he became a role model for the republic, and Abraham Lincoln had to overcome deep melancholia to display the brave and warm countenance that made him a magnet for others. Franklin Delano Roosevelt provides an even more graphic example: In his early adult years, FDR seemed carefree and condescending. Then, at 39, he was stricken with polio. By most accounts, he transformed himself over the next seven years of struggle into a leader of empathy, patience, and keen self-awareness.

Richard Nixon thought he might transform himself through his own years in the wilderness, and he did make progress. But he could never fully control his demons, and they eventually brought him down. Bill Clinton, too, has struggled for self-mastery and has made progress, but he could not fully close the cracks in his character, and he paid a stiff price. Not all people suc-ceed, then, in achieving self-awareness and self-control.

What we have been told since the time of the Greeks is that every leader must try to control his own passions before he can hope to command the passions of others.

Best-selling author Rabbi Harold Kushner argues persuasively that the elements of selfishness and aggression that are in most of us—and our struggles to overcome them—are exactly what make for better leadership. In *Living a Life That Matters,* Kushner writes of the personal torments of leaders from Jacob, who wrestled all night with an angel, to Martin Luther King, Jr., who tried to cleanse himself of weakness even as he cleansed the nation's soul. "Good people do bad things," Kushner concludes, "If they weren't mightily tempted by their *yetzer ha'ra* [will to do evil], they might not be capable of the mightily good things they do."

Let Your Guard Down

Sidney Harman (sharman@harman.com) is the executive chairman and founder of Harman International Industries in Washington, DC.

Eight years ago, we acquired Becker Radio (now Harman/Becker) to help us develop the dashboard navigation and media systems that are now the major part of our business. In a meeting at Becker, several of the engineers there argued that the only way for us to take the lead in the emerging field of "infotainment" was to abandon tried-and-true analog systems and design and build totally new digital systems—a very risky proposition for our company.

Back home, I sat down with our key executives to talk about this disruptive idea. I went into the meeting with only a rough notion of how we should proceed. There was clearly anxiety and skepticism in the group, concern that we would be betting the company if we went digital. I realized that to provoke the creative thinking we needed, I would have to let my guard down and be willing to embarrass myself by floating unformed—and even uninformed—ideas. I assured the group that anything we said in the meeting stayed with us. Our discussion went on for six or seven hours. By opening up to my colleagues, and by encouraging them to think freely and improvise, I helped generate a novel perspective that no one of us had brought to the meeting: Commit all the company's resources to this digital direction, facilitate the transformation by eliminating hierarchies and silos, and remove barriers between functions.

Today, our sales are approaching $3 billion, and our stock price is at an all-time high. We wouldn't be here if we hadn't taken the radical steps conceived in that meeting. And that plan would not have emerged had I failed to recognize and respond to the group's apprehension and elicit its collective creative thinking. The leader who uses emotional intelligence to catalyze creative thinking subordinates himself to the team but elevates the company to achieve goals it otherwise couldn't.

Watch Your Culture

Janja Lalich (jlalich@csuchico.edu) is an assistant professor of sociology at California State University, Chico, and an expert on cults.

Cult leaders don't do anything mysterious; they just know how to package themselves and their promises well and how to target responsive audiences.

They're very good at influencing, or, to be more precise, manipulating, followers. To do this, they rely on a keen ability to perceive others' vulnerabilities and longings— to know what people want.

One way a cult leader manipulates is by exploiting followers' eagerness to be part of something bigger than themselves. That desire often prompts followers to assign to a leader attributes that he doesn't actually possess. A type of group contagion can take hold—a "true-believerism" mentality. Then followers can fall into what I call uncritical obedience, never questioning the leader's claims. When followers give a leader this power, there are obvious dangers.

Cult leaders are also skillful at convincing followers that the leader's ideas are their own. Once followers own the ideas, it's difficult for them to extricate themselves from the leader's message. For example, a leader may exaggerate his own importance. In the 1980s, Bhagwan Shree Rajneesh, a wildly popular Oregon-based Eastern guru, always surrounded himself with armed guards. That heightened sense of need for security led some of his followers to perform dangerous, antisocial activities in their desire to protect and defend their ashram and Rajneesh himself.

Cult leaders also make it difficult for people to leave. They set up interlocking systems of influence and control that keep followers obedient and prevent them from thinking about their own needs. Cult leaders may offer "rewards"—sometimes material, more often ephemeral—that keep followers committed to the leader and to the organization's goals. The differences between how a conventional leader influences followers and how cult leaders manipulate them can be subtle. Sometimes the only difference is their intent. And sometimes there is no difference.

Find Your Voice

William George *is the former chairman and CEO of Medtronic, a medical technology company in Minneapolis.*

AUTHENTIC LEADERSHIP BEGINS with self-awareness, or knowing yourself deeply. Self-awareness is not a trait you are born with but a capacity you develop throughout your lifetime. It's your understanding of your strengths and weaknesses, your purpose in life, your values and motivations, and how and why you respond to situations in a particular way. It requires a great deal of introspection and the ability to internalize feedback from others.

No one is born a leader; we have to consciously develop into the leader we want to become. It takes many years of hard work and the ability to learn from extreme difficulties and disappointments. But in their scramble to get ahead, many would-be leaders attempt to skip this crucial developmental stage. Some of these people do get to the top of companies through sheer determination and aggressiveness. However, when they finally reach the leader's chair, they can be very destructive because they haven't focused on the hard work of personal development.

To mask their inadequacies, these leaders tend to close themselves off, cultivating an image or persona rather than opening up to others. They often adopt the styles of other leaders they have observed.

Leaders who are driven to achieve by shortcomings in their character, for example, or a desire for self-aggrandizement, may take inordinate risks on behalf of the organization. They may even come to believe they are so important that they place their interests above those of the organization.

Self-awareness and other emotional intelligence skills come naturally to some, less so to others—but these skills can be learned. One of the techniques I have found most useful in gaining deeper self-awareness is meditation. In 1975, my wife dragged me, kicking and screaming, to a weekend course in Transcendental Meditation. I have meditated 20 minutes, twice a day, ever since. Meditation makes me calmer, more focused, and better able to discern what's really important. Leaders, by the very nature of their positions, are under extreme pressure to keep up with the many voices clamoring for their attention. Indeed, many leaders lose their way. It is only through a deep self-awareness that you can find your inner voice and listen to it.

Know the Score

Michael Tilson Thomas is the music director of the San Francisco Symphony.

A conductor's authority rests on two things: the orchestra's confidence in the conductor's insightful knowledge of the whole score; and the orchestra's faith in the conductor's good heart, which seeks to inspire everyone to make music that is excellent, generous, and sincere.

Old-school conductors liked to hold the lead in their hands at all times. I do not. Sometimes I lead. Other times I'll say, "Violas, I'm giving you the lead. Listen to one another, and find your way with this phrase." I'm not trying to drill people, military style, to play music exactly together. I'm trying to encourage them to play as one, which is a different thing. I'm guiding the performance, but I'm aware that they're executing it. It's their sinews, their heartstrings. I'm there to help them do it in a way that is convincing and natural for them but also a part of the larger design.

My approach is to be in tune with the people with whom I'm working. If I'm conducting an ensemble for the first time, I will relate what it is I want them to do to the great things they've already done. If I'm conducting my own orchestra, I can see in the musicians' bodies and faces how they're feeling that day, and it becomes very clear who may need encouragement and who may need cautioning.

The objectivity and perspective I have as the only person who is just listening is a powerful thing. I try to use this perspective to help the ensemble reach its goals.

Keep It Honest

Carol Bartz (carol.bartz@autodesk.com) is the chairman, president, and CEO of Autodesk, a design software and digital content company in San Rafael, California.

A FRIEND NEEDED TO TAKE a six-month assignment in a different part of the country. She had an ancient, ill, balding but beloved dog that she could not take with her. Her choices boiled down to boarding the poor animal, at enormous expense, or putting it out of its obvious misery. Friends said, "Board the dog," though behind my friend's back, they ridiculed that option. She asked me what I thought, and I told her, kindly but clearly, that I thought she should have the dog put to sleep rather than spend her money keeping it in an environment where it would be miserable and perhaps die anyway. My friend was furious with me for saying this. She boarded the dog and went away on her assignment. When she returned, the dog was at death's door and had to be put to sleep. Not long after that, my friend came around to say thanks. "You were the only person who told me the truth," she said. She came to appreciate that I had cared enough to tell her what I thought was best, even if what I said hurt at the time.

That event validated a hunch that has stood me in good stead as I've led my company. Empathy and compassion have to be balanced with honesty. I have pulled people into my office and told them to deal with certain issues for the sake of themselves and their teams. If they are willing to learn, they will say, "Gee, no one ever told me." If they are unwilling, they're not right for this organization. And I must let them go for the sake of the greater good.

Go for the *Gemba*

Hirotaka Takeuchi is the dean of Hitotsubashi University's Graduate School of International Corporate Strategy in Tokyo.

SELF-AWARENESS, SELF-CONTROL, empathy, humility, and other such emotional intelligence traits are particularly important in Asia. They are part of our Confucian emphasis on *wah,* or social harmony. When books on emotional intelligence were first translated into Japanese, people said, "We already know that. We're actually trying to get beyond that." We've been so

focused on wah that we've built up a supersensitive
structure of social niceties, where everyone seeks con-
sensus. In the Japanese hierarchy, everyone knows his or
her place so no one is ever humiliated. This social super-
sensitivity—itself a form of emotional intelligence—can
lead people to shy away from conflict. But conflict is
often the only way to get to the *gemba*—the front line,
where the action really is, where the truth lies.

Thus, effective management often depends not on
coolly and expertly resolving conflict, or simply avoiding
it, but on embracing it at the gemba. Japan's most effective leaders do both. The best example is Nissan's Carlos
Ghosn. He not only had the social skills to listen to people and win them over to his ideas, but he also dared to
lift the lid on the corporate hierarchy and encourage people at all levels of the organization to offer suggestions to
operational, organizational, and even interpersonal
problems—even if that created conflict. People were no
longer suppressed, so solutions to the company's problems bubbled up.

Balance the Load

*Linda Stone (linda@lindastone.net) is the former vice
president of corporate and industry initiatives at
Microsoft in Redmond, Washington.*

Emotional intelligence is powerful—which
is precisely why it can be dangerous. For example, empathy is an extraordinary relationship-building tool, but it
must be used skillfully or it can do serious damage to the
person doing the empathizing. In my case, overdoing
empathy took a physical toll. In May 2000, Steve Ballmer

charged me with rebuilding Microsoft's industry relationships, a position that I sometimes referred to as chief listening officer. The job was part ombudsperson, part new-initiatives developer, part pattern recognizer, and part rapid-response person. In the first few months of the job—when criticism of the company was at an all-time high—it became clear that this position was a lightning rod. I threw myself into listening and repairing wherever I could.

Within a few months, I was exhausted from the effort. I gained a significant amount of weight, which, tests finally revealed, was probably caused by a hormone imbalance partially brought on by stress and lack of sleep. In absorbing everyone's complaints, perhaps to the extreme, I had compromised my health. This was a wake-up call; I needed to reframe the job.

I focused on connecting the people who needed to work together to resolve problems rather than taking on each repair myself. I persuaded key people inside the company to listen and work directly with important people outside the company, even in cases where the internal folks were skeptical at first about the need for this direct connection. In a sense, I tempered my empathy and ratcheted up relationship building. Ultimately, with a wiser and more balanced use of empathy, I became more effective and less stressed in my role.

Question Authority

Ronald Heifetz (ronald_heifetz@harvard.edu) is a cofounder of the Center for Public Leadership at Harvard University's John F. Kennedy School of Government in Cambridge, Massachusetts, and a partner at Cambridge Leadership Associates, a consultancy in Cambridge.

Eмотional intelligence is necessary for leadership but not sufficient. Many people have some degree of emotional intelligence and can indeed empathize with and rouse followers; a few of them can even generate great charismatic authority. But I would argue that if they are using emotional intelligence solely to gain formal or informal authority, that's not leadership at all. They are using their emotional intelligence to grasp what people want, only to pander to those desires in order to gain authority and influence. Easy answers sell.

Leadership couples emotional intelligence with the courage to raise the tough questions, challenge people's assumptions about strategy and operations—and risk losing their goodwill. It demands a commitment to serving others; skill at diagnostic, strategic, and tactical reasoning; the guts to get beneath the surface of tough realities; and the heart to take heat and grief.

For example, David Duke did an extraordinary job of convincing Ku Klux Klan members to get out of their backyards and into hotel conference rooms. He brought his considerable emotional intelligence to bear, his capacity to empathize with his followers, to pluck their heartstrings in a powerful way that mobilized them. But he avoided asking his people the tough questions: Does our program actually solve our problem? How will creating a social structure of white supremacy give us the self-esteem we lack? How will it solve the problems of poverty, alcoholism, and family violence that corrode our sense of self-worth?

Like Duke, many people with high emotional intelligence and charismatic authority aren't interested in asking the deeper questions, because they get so much emotional gain from the adoring crowd. For them, that's the end in itself. They're satisfying their own hungers and vulnerabilities: their need to be liked; their need for power and control; or their need to be needed, to feel important, which renders them vulnerable to grandiosity. But that's not primal leadership. It's primal hunger for authority.

Maintaining one's primacy or position is not, in and of itself, leadership, however inspiring it may seem to be. Gaining primal authority is relatively easy.

Originally published in January 2004
Reprint R0401B

The Dangers of
Feeling like a Fake

MANFRED F. R. KETS DE VRIES

Executive Summary

IN MANY WALKS OF LIFE—and business is no exception—there are high achievers who believe that they are
complete fakes. To the outside observer, these individuals appear to be remarkably accomplished; often they
are extremely successful leaders with staggering lists of
achievements.

These *neurotic impostors*—as psychologists call them—
are not guilty of false humility. The sense of being a fraud
is the flip side of giftedness and causes a great many talented, hardworking, and capable leaders to believe that
they don't deserve their success. "Bluffing" their way
through life (as they see it), they are haunted by the constant fear of exposure. With every success, they think, "I
was lucky *this* time, fooling everyone, but will my luck
hold? When will people discover that I'm not up to
the job?"

In his career as a management professor, consultant, leadership coach, and psychoanalyst, Manfred F. R. Kets de Vries has found neurotic impostors at all levels of organizations. In this article, he explores the subject of neurotic imposture and outlines its classic symptoms: fear of failure, fear of success, perfectionism, procrastination, and workaholism. He then describes how perfectionist overachievers can damage their careers, their colleagues' morale, and the bottom line by allowing anxiety to trigger self-handicapping behavior and cripple the very organizations they're trying so hard to please. Finally, Kets de Vries offers advice on how to limit the incidence of neurotic imposture and mitigate its damage through discreet vigilance, appropriate intervention, and constructive support.

A FEW YEARS AGO, a middle manager in a telecommunications company came to see me upon his promotion to a senior management role. I'll call him Tobin Holmes (all case study names in this article have been disguised). A young Englishman who had studied classics at Oxford before graduating in the top 5% of his class at Insead, Holmes was very clever. But he feared he couldn't take on the new job's responsibilities. At the root of Holmes's dilemma was his suspicion that he was just not good enough, and he lived in dread that he would be exposed at any moment. Yet, at the same time, he seemed bent on betraying the very inadequacy he was so anxious to conceal. In his personal life, for example, he indulged in conspicuously self-destructive behavior, such as public affairs with numerous women and a drinking spree that resulted in a disastrous car accident. At work, he found it increasingly difficult to concentrate and make decisions. He worried—and now for good reason— that his problems at the office would be noticed by the CEO and other members of the board. When would they realize that they had made a horrible mistake in promoting him to the senior executive team?

When the fear and stress overwhelmed him, Holmes quit his job and accepted a junior position at a larger organization. Given his genuine talent, however, it didn't take long before he was asked to head up one of that company's major country units, a role widely known to be a stepping-stone to the top. In this new role, Holmes's feelings of doubt resurfaced. Rather than risk being exposed as incompetent, he left the job within a year and moved on to yet another company. There, despite his performance, top management looked at his employment record and concluded that Holmes just didn't have the right stuff to make it to the highest levels of leadership.

Holmes couldn't let himself move up to the most senior levels in an organization because, deep inside, he feared that he was an impostor who would eventually be discovered. In many walks of life—and business is no exception—there are high achievers who believe that they are complete fakes. To the outside observer, these individuals appear to be remarkably accomplished; often they are extremely successful leaders. Despite their staggering achievements, however, these people subjectively sense that they are frauds. This *neurotic imposture,* as psychologists call it, is not a false humility. It is the flip side of giftedness and causes many talented, hardworking, and capable leaders—men and women who have achieved great things—to believe that they don't deserve their success.

To some extent, of course, we are *all* impostors. We play roles on the stage of life, presenting a public self that differs from the private self we share with intimates and morphing both selves as circumstances demand. Displaying a facade is part and parcel of the human condition. Indeed, one reason the feeling of being an impostor is so widespread is that society places enormous pressure on people to stifle their real selves.

But neurotic impostors feel more fraudulent and alone than other people do. Because they view themselves as charlatans, their success is worse than meaningless: It is a burden. In their heart of hearts, these self-doubters believe that others are much smarter and more capable than they are, so any praise impostors earn makes no sense to them. "Bluffing" their way through life (as they see it), they are haunted by the constant fear of exposure. With every success, they think, "I was lucky this time, fooling everyone, but will my luck hold? When will people discover that I'm not up to the job?"

Neurotic impostors can be found at all levels of an organization. Typically, the misgivings begin with the first job, right after graduation, when people are fraught with anxiety and particularly insecure about their ability to prove themselves. Promotion from middle management to senior management is another tricky time because an executive must negotiate the difficult switch from being a specialist to becoming a general manager. But neurotic impostors face their greatest challenges when they are promoted from senior management to CEO. In my work with senior managers and CEOs, I've found that many neurotic impostors function well as long as they aren't in the number one position. Often, a leader's feelings of self-doubt and anxiety are less pressing when he is lower on the totem pole, because senior executives usually provide support and mentoring. But once a leader becomes the CEO, everything he does is highly visible. He is expected to stand on his own.

For this reason, people like Tobin Holmes abound in business. In my career as a management professor, consultant, leadership coach, and psychoanalyst, I have explored the topic of neurotic imposture with individuals and with large groups of senior executives. My experience has shown that feelings of neurotic imposture proliferate in today's organizations, and I encounter this type of dysfunctional perception and behavior all the time—particularly when working with executives in consulting firms and in investment banking. In the following pages, I will describe the phenomenon of neurotic imposture; explore how perfectionist overachievers can damage their careers by allowing their anxiety to trigger self-handicapping behavior; and discuss how such an executive's dysfunctional behavior can have a ripple effect throughout a company, hurting not just the morale of colleagues but also the bottom line.

Why You Might Feel like a Fake

The term *impostor phenomenon* was coined in 1978 by Georgia State University psychology professor Pauline Clance and psychologist Suzanne Imes in a study of high-achieving women. These psychologists discovered that many of their female clients seemed unable to internalize and accept their achievements. Instead, in spite of consistent objective data to the contrary, they attributed their successes to serendipity, luck, contacts, timing, perseverance, charm, or even the ability to appear more capable than they felt themselves to be. (See the insert "Women and the Impostor Phenomenon" at the end of this article.)

Numerous doctoral theses and research papers have
followed that original study. Although their findings
have not always been consistent, most studies suggest
that neurotic imposture is by no means limited to
women. Men can also exhibit it—though, interestingly,
genuine imposture (that is, deliberate fraud) is more
common in men than in women (see the insert "Genuine
Fakes" at the end of this article). Further, the incidence
of neurotic imposture seems to vary by profession. For
example, it is highly prevalent in academia and medicine,
both disciplines in which the appearance of intelligence
is vital to success.

Not surprisingly, my clinical interviews with CEOs
and other high-level executives suggest that specific family structures can be breeding grounds for feelings of
imposture. Certain dysfunctional families—particularly
those in which parents are overinvested in achievement
and where human warmth is lacking—tend to produce
children who are prone to neurotic imposture. Individuals who have been raised in this kind of environment
seem to believe that their parents will notice them only
when they excel. As time goes on, these people often turn
into insecure overachievers.

Paradoxically, a predisposition to neurotic imposture
is also quite common in individuals who are *not*
expected to succeed. In socially disadvantaged groups
(often with a blue-collar background, for example), parents may withhold encouragement because their children's ambitions are inconsistent with family expectations. Children who manage to advance to positions of
real power as adults, however, often transcend their families of origin in such a spectacular way that a lingering
insecurity remains about having become so "grandiose"

in their success. Frequently, because of conflicting signals, these executives wonder just how long that success will last. This fear of surpassing one's parents can cause feelings of neurotic imposture to persist long after the parents have died.

Birth order also influences the development of neurotic imposture. Feelings of imposture are more common among firstborn children, reflecting the new parents' nervous inexperience and greater expectations of these children. For example, older children are often expected to help out in the care of brothers and sisters and are held up to younger siblings as models of maturity.

How Your Fear Becomes Reality

How does neurotic imposture get out of hand? The trigger is often perfectionism. In its mild form, of course, perfectionism provides the energy that leads to great accomplishments. "Benign" perfectionists, who do not suffer feelings of inadequacy, derive pleasure from their achievements and don't obsess over failures. Neurotic impostors, however, are seldom benign in their perfectionism. They are "absolute" perfectionists, who set excessively high, unrealistic goals and then experience self-defeating thoughts and behaviors when they can't reach those goals. They are driven by the belief that they are currently not good enough, but that they could do better if only they worked harder. For this reason, perfectionism often turns neurotic impostors into workaholics. Fearing discovery of their "fraudulence," they burden themselves with too much work to compensate for their lack of self-esteem and identity. Work/life balance is a meaningless concept to them.

I'm reminded of a cartoon that depicts a CEO handing over a dossier to one of his subordinates. He says, "Take your time. I'm not in a hurry. Take the whole weekend if necessary." Neurotic impostors commonly enter into abusive, self-defeating collusions of this sort. They don't realize that they may be pushing themselves and others too hard, often to the detriment of long-term success. By exploiting themselves so brutally in this way, they risk rapid and early burnout.

The vicious cycle begins when the impostor sets impossible goals. She fails to reach these goals, of course (because *no one* could reach them), then tortures herself endlessly about the failure, which incites further self-flagellation, accentuates the feelings of imposture, and inspires her to designate yet another unattainable set of goals—and the entire cycle of workaholism and fraudulence begins again. That's what happened to Robert Pierce, an extraordinarily gifted trader at a highly prestigious investment bank, who set ever increasing goals of financial compensation for himself to deal with his anxieties about being a fake. Initially, Pierce felt elated whenever he reached his goal; but he became more desperate every time he learned that someone else earned more than he did. This kicked off an orgy of self-blame that did little to improve his career or his organizational effectiveness.

When Fakes Court Failure

Because they are so ambivalent about their achievements, neurotic impostors often appear to be engagingly humble. Self-deprecation, of course, is a perfectly respectable character trait and, from a career management point of view, can be seen as a protective strategy. Underplaying one's achievements defuses other people's envy and directs attention away from success, thereby lowering others' expectations—a useful maneuver in case of future failure. A display of self-deprecation also seems to convey a sense of modesty, which can elicit encouragement and support from others.

But the neurotic impostor's humility actually stems from another kind of protective impulse: the need for an exit strategy. Failure (at least at a subliminal level) becomes a desirable way out. Think of the journalist who wins a Pulitzer prize at a relatively young age. Such a "gift" can turn out to be a poisonous boon. When such good fortune occurs, what can one do for an encore? Great achievements have ruined many a neurotic impostor because they can lead to paralysis. Indeed, to neurotic impostors, granting wishes for success can be one of fate's cruelest jokes.

For many neurotic impostors, the heart of the problem is the fear that success and fame will hurt them in some way—that family, friends, and others will continue to like them much better if they remain "small." After all, people who covet success are likely to envy those who have achieved it. As Ambrose Bierce wrote in *The Devil's Dictionary,* success is "the one unpardonable sin against one's fellows."

In extreme cases, neurotic impostors bring about the very failure that they fear. This self-destructive behavior can take many forms, including procrastination, abrasiveness, and the inability to delegate. As Tobin Holmes's experience illustrates, it can also take such extreme forms as inappropriate womanizing or substance abuse on the job.

Neurotic impostors are also quite creative at destroying their own successful careers. It's as if they *want* to be discovered. Perhaps assisting in their own unmasking is a proactive way of coping with their anxiety; maybe it offers a sense of relief.

Mike Larson, a senior executive I worked with a few years ago, exemplifies this propensity. After a brilliant career as a medical researcher, Larson was offered the position of director of research in a global company specializing in over-the-counter drugs. When he embarked on this challenging new research agenda, however, Larson's incessant fear of exposure harmed rather than enhanced his performance. It was one thing to be a member of a team, but taking on the number one research position was another question altogether. To be so visible made him feel increasingly anxious, contributing to his drive to do even better; but his inability to delegate and his tendency toward micromanagement led to a greater sense of malaise.

Larson realized that he was digging a hole for himself, but it was difficult for him to ask for help. He was afraid that doing so would give his colleagues proof of what they surely suspected—that he was an impostor, a fraud. To avoid being found out, he withdrew into himself, agonized over what his colleagues thought about him, worried about not living up to their expectations, and waffled over every decision. The result was anxiety-filled days, sleepless nights, and an intense fear of making mistakes—a fear that made him unwilling to experiment, develop, and learn.

Like most neurotic impostors, Larson engaged in faulty reality testing. This distortion in his cognition caused him to dramatize all setbacks—he blew small incidents out of proportion and cast himself as the helpless victim. Larson lived with the misconception that he was the only one prone to failure and self-doubt, and this made him feel even more insecure and isolated. Like other neurotic impostors, he focused on the negative and failed to give himself credit for his accomplishments. He also harmed his career by becoming a master of catastrophizing—reaching exaggerated conclusions based on limited evidence.

Only when Larson was awarded the top research position did he realize how much he missed the mentors he'd had at earlier stages of his career. Those mentors had helped him to deal with the pressures of his job and to maintain equilibrium under stress. But when he was promoted, he found it much harder to ask for advice and to find people who would challenge his faulty cognition. As a result, he executed a number of poor management decisions that contributed to his organization's ineffectiveness. Eventually, he was asked to step down from the director's position.

The Neurotic Organization

Neurotic impostors can, and do, damage the organizations they try so hard to please. Their work ethic can be contagious, but because they are so eager to succeed, they often become impatient and abrasive. Neurotic impostors are extremely tough on themselves and thus not predisposed to spare others. They drive their employees too hard and create a gulag-like atmosphere in their organizations, which inevitably translates into high employee turnover rates, absenteeism, and other complications that can affect the bottom line. Moreover, neurotic impostors can intimidate others with their intensity. And because they don't have what it takes to be effective leadership coaches, they are not generally talented in leadership development and succession planning.

More dangerous, however, is neurotic imposture's effect on the quality of decision making. Executives who feel like impostors are afraid to trust their own judgment. Their fearful, overly cautious kind of leadership can easily spread across the company and bring about dire consequences for the organization. For instance, a neurotic impostor CEO is very likely to suppress his company's entrepreneurial capabilities. After all, if he doesn't trust his own instincts, why should he trust anyone else's?

Neurotic impostor CEOs are also highly likely to become addicted to consulting companies because reassurances provided by "impartial" outsiders compensate for the executives' feelings of insecurity. Of course, judicious use of consulting advice does have its place; but neurotic impostor executives all too easily turn into puppets whose strings are completely manipulated by those same advisers. Ralph Gordon, the CEO of a global engineering firm, suffered just such an experience. In a group session during one of my seminars, he explained that he really didn't choose engineering—his father had chosen it for him. Gordon conceded to his father's wishes and entered the business world, where he never felt comfortable in his corporate role. When he reached more senior positions, Gordon began to rely on consultants, some of whom took advantage of his insecurity at a very high price. Not only did they charge Gordon's firm substantial fees for their services, but their predatory behavior increased Gordon's feelings of dependency.

This type of behavior is exacerbated when neurotic impostors work in an organization that punishes failure.

If the company culture does not tolerate mistakes, the leader's level of anxiety will increase, making neurotic behavior all the more likely. This is paralyzing for the perfectionist whose fear of failure will have an even more negative impact on the organization.

Consider Lynn Orwell, who had a successful career at a consulting firm before accepting an offer from a prominent media company. In her consulting job, Orwell had functioned exceptionally well. But this changed when she accepted an assignment to run the new firm's European operation.

Although Orwell was an outstanding source of good ideas, her fear of failure led her to manage in ways that seemed countercultural. In an organization that had always been decentralized, for example, she decided to centralize many of the functions in her part of the business. But what really grated on many people was that Orwell wanted to make most of the decisions herself. Her perfectionist attitude and her need for immediate results made delegation anathema to her and dampened the team's productivity and creativity. Orwell's coworkers started to worry about the abrasiveness that had crept into her manner, and her prickliness about criticism— whether real or perceived—began to irritate a growing number of her colleagues. She reacted with defensiveness and hostility to comments about any of her proposals, reports, or decisions. Furthermore, anxious not to be found wanting, she took ages to prepare for meetings, trying to anticipate every conceivable question that could be asked. Such precautions extended her already lengthy workweek into weekends, and she expected others to show the same commitment.

Orwell's sense of neurotic imposture deeply affected the organization. As time went on, many of Orwell's team members began to ask for transfers to other parts of the organization. Others quietly sought out head-hunters. Those who stayed took a passive-aggressive attitude toward Orwell. Since they felt it was not worth the effort to reason with her, they let her make all the decisions but undermined them in subtle ways. As a result, her European division—once hailed as the flagship operation—was increasingly seen as a liability. By the year's end, profitability for Orwell's division had fallen into a deep slump, confirming the company's belief that she was truly incompetent. Ultimately, the division was sold to a competitor. Orwell's neurosis had ruined not only her career but a perfectly robust business as well.

The Light at the End of the Tunnel

Neurotic imposture is not an inevitable part of the human condition, and it is avoidable. Early prevention, for instance, can completely ward it off. If caregivers identify and deal with factors that lead to this phenomenon very early in life, the dysfunctional effects will never surface. Parental awareness of the downside of setting excessively high standards for children goes a long way toward preventing later misery. But there is hope for late-diagnosed impostors as well. Experience has shown that psychotherapeutic interventions can be very effective in changing distorted self-perceptions.

Yet the best—and often most appropriate—way for you to manage feelings of imposture can be to evaluate yourself. After all, you are the best person to assess the source of these problems. And though a leadership coach or psychotherapist can certainly help you on this journey of self-discovery and change, a mentor or good friend can also put things in perspective. Realizing that you may repeat with your children the same pattern of behavior you learned from your parents, for instance, can be a great motivator.

If you are unable to take the initiative to deal with your feelings of imposture, however, your boss needs to intervene. Such was the case with John Stodard, the CEO of a large telecommunications company, who came to talk to me upon the recommendation of his chairman. In our sessions, Stodard wondered if he needed pointers on how to be a more effective executive. A 360-degree feedback exercise showed that he was inclined toward micromanagement and perfectionism and that he possessed poor listening skills. Some of the written comments also noted that his impatience put intense pressure on his directors and that morale at the office was quite low. As we discussed the problem together, Stodard began to realize the extent to which he had internalized the expectations of his extremely demanding parents, and he started to change. He began to experiment with new behavior in the office and received a surprisingly positive reception, which increased his sense of self-efficacy. When I met him a year later, Stodard mentioned quite proudly how morale at the office had dramatically improved, how the company had become more profitable, and how his ability to let go of his controlling tendencies had contributed to these successes.

Like Stodard's chairman, good bosses remain alert for symptoms of neurotic imposture in their employees: fear of failure, fear of success, perfectionism, procrastination, and workaholism. In performance reviews, bosses should signal (uncritically) any danger signs to their direct reports. They should also explain how anxiety about performance can take on a self-destructive quality, and they should emphasize the value of work/life balance, pointing out that extreme strength can easily become a weakness.

Above all, bosses need to make sure that a subordinate suffering from neurotic imposture understands that with responsibility comes constructive criticism. This means teaching—by word and by example—that open, honest, critical feedback is an opportunity for new learning and not an irredeemable catastrophe. They must point out that *everyone* in a responsible job occasionally feels unequal to the task and needs time to adjust and learn the ropes. The worst thing a neurotic impostor can do, especially in a new position, is to compare his abilities with those of seasoned executives. This is guaranteed to be an exercise in self-flagellation.

At the same time, leaders must strengthen the perceived link between positive achievements and efforts. They can do this not only by offering praise when it's due, but also by acknowledging that making mistakes (though not repeating them!) is part of a successful corporate culture. The wise organization does not punish "smart" mistakes; indeed, to "fail forward" should be part of an organization's implicit cultural values. Mistakes can offer great opportunities for learning and personal growth, and leaders need to help neurotic impostors understand that a fear of failure is normal and need not be debilitating.

When it's the CEO himself who feels like a neurotic impostor, the situation is more complicated. A leader at the top does not find it easy to ask for support from mentors or from subordinates who feel their boss "has it all." For this reason, many high-performance organizations now have leadership-coaching programs to help their executives cope better with the vicissitudes of working life. When leadership coaches recognize the signs of neurotic imposture, they are in a good position to give constructive advice. In the 15 years that I have been running top-level seminars at Insead, I have listened to executives discuss significant experiences in their work and personal lives. Being willing to talk about these neurotic imposture problems and accept peer support not only has a profound effect on leaders but also has a deep impact on the organization that the neurotic impostor has helped to shape.

It's often said that a person's strengths are also his weaknesses. The same is true for an organization. In most well-run organizations, senior managers remove low performers or develop them to become high performers. But these same managers are less effective in managing people who appear to be problem-free. By their very nature, neurotic impostors are very hard to detect because the early stages of an executive's career are so conducive to high performance. It is, in fact, a rare leader who does not suffer from neurotic imposture. All the more reason, therefore, for managers to be on the lookout for it in themselves, their reports, and their potential successors. Failing to recognize and deal with neurotic impostors has serious consequences both for individual sufferers and for the organizations relying on them.

Women and the Impostor Phenomenon

WOMEN WHO REACH SUCCESSFUL POSITIONS that conflict with their family of origin's way of thinking about gender roles are especially prone to feeling fraudulent. The gender socialization that women are often exposed to—for instance, being told that they should become nurses or secretaries when choosing a career—tends to augment their sense of imposture when their achievements rise above those expectations. Ironically, this feeling might, at an unconscious level, carry benefits: A woman might be able to deal with ambivalence about her real career achievements by keeping them out of conscious awareness.

Inner confusion develops into genuine neurotic imposture for many women when they reach critical junctures in their lives concerning marriage, work, and children. These decisions are especially difficult for women who have had traditional mothers. Consciously or not, women tend to compare their chosen roles with the roles their mothers played. The fact that working women choose not to stay at home but rather to pursue a career—a lifestyle so different from what they witnessed as children—often makes them feel like bad mothers to their own children and bad wives to their husbands.

Gender role socialization isn't the only thing that makes women more vulnerable than men to neurotic imposture. The fact that businesswomen have to function in an environment dominated by men compounds their insecurity, because when women are successful, they're not the only ones who suspect imposture. Many of their competitive male colleagues likewise assume that chance or an affirmative action program—not talent or skill—was responsible for the success. Though few men will express such an opinion publicly, subtle insinuations from male colleagues add to a woman's fear that the "luck" won't last. As a result, many very gifted women don't know that they have superior talents. Moreover, if they do realize it, they are more likely than men to hide those talents and to play dumb as a strategy for dealing with others' envy and their own recurring feelings of self-doubt.

Genuine Fakes

IN CONTRAST TO NEUROTIC IMPOSTORS, true impostors are con artists—and they tend to be men. Consider Ferdinand Waldo Demara, for example. In the fall of 1951, this real impostor's career came to an abrupt halt after a woman became alarmed by an article she saw in her daily newspaper. The article described a successful emergency operation performed by Joseph Cyr, a surgeon, on the deck of a Royal Canadian Navy destroyer during the Korean War. Worried, the woman contacted her son, also a physician named Joseph Cyr, who assured her that he was safe and sound and practicing medicine in New Brunswick. Unsettled by the odd coincidence of names, however, Dr. Cyr then contacted the police, an initiative that led to the unraveling of Demara's bizarre career.

It didn't take long for the authorities to find out that Demara was masquerading as Dr. Cyr. In fact, the bogus doctor's medical "training" had been limited to a few weeks working as an unskilled hospital orderly in the United States. That experience, however, along with the help of the ship's medical attendant and the navy's generous supply of anesthetics and antibiotics, was enough for him to successfully play the role of medical doctor. Fortunately, despite Demara's lack of qualifications, his patients survived their treatments.

Further investigation revealed that Demara had gone through most of his life masquerading as other people.

His career as an impostor spanned three decades and included a wide variety of pseudo-identities, such as deputy sheriff, prison warden, psychologist, university lecturer, Trappist monk, and cancer researcher. This chameleon-like career didn't come without a price, however. At one point, Demara's impersonation resulted in a term of imprisonment.

Apparently, his inability to figure out what to do with his life motivated him to masquerade as other people, with the professed hope of eventually "finding" himself. Personal gain wasn't a major part of the equation. Interestingly enough, his talent at playing different roles was remarkable, and many of his unsuspecting employers were quite satisfied with his work. He was a master of improvisation, gathering from textbooks and observation the necessary knowledge to fill each role he took on.

Demara's exploits fascinated the public. After his discharge from the Canadian navy, he sold his story to *Life* magazine and became the subject of a book by Robert Crichton, which led to the making of the film *The Great Impostor,* starring Tony Curtis. Crichton reported that he'd had a hard time pinning down the impostor's motives for engaging in all his masquerades. At one point, Demara is said to have told him, "I'm a rotten man," adding that he was prompted by "rascality, sheer rascality." But Demara also suggested that his activities served a good cause. According to him, his various impostures were instrumental in making organizations more vigilant about confidential records, thereby helping to better secure people's privacy.

Originally published in September 2005
Reprint R0509F

About the Contributors

COLLEEN BARRETT is the president and corporate secretary of Dallas-based Southwest Airlines.

CAROL BARTZ is the executive chairman of the board of Autodesk, a design software and digital content company in San Rafael, California. She is also a member of President Bush's Council of Advisors on Science and Technology.

HERBERT BENSON, MD, is the director emeritus of the Benson-Henry Institute (BHI), and Mind/Body Medical Institute Associate Professor of Medicine, Harvard Medical School.

HOWARD BOOK is an associate professor in the department of psychiatry at the University of Toronto and an organizational consultant.

RICHARD BOYATZIS is a professor and the chair of the department of organizational behavior at Case Western Reserve University's Weatherhead School of Management in Cleveland.

CHARLES A. CZEISLER is the Baldino Professor of Sleep Medicine at Harvard Medical School.

BRONWYN FRYER is a senior editor at *Harvard Business Review*.

WILLIAM GEORGE is the former chairman and CEO of Medtronic, a medical technology company in Minneapolis. He is currently professor of management practice, Henry B. Arthur Fellow of Ethics, at Harvard Business School.

DAVID GERGEN directs the Center for Public Leadership at Harvard University's John F. Kennedy School of Government in Cambridge, Massachusetts. He served as an adviser to presidents Nixon, Ford, Reagan, and Clinton.

ROBERT GOFFEE is a professor of organizational behavior at London Business School and a cofounder of Creative Management Associates, an organizational consulting firm in London.

ELKHONON GOLDBERG is a clinical professor of neurology at New York University School of Medicine and the director of the Institute of Neuropsychology and Cognitive Performance in New York.

DANIEL GOLEMAN is the cochair of the Consortium for Research on Emotional Intelligence in Organizations based at Rutgers University's Graduate School of Applied and Professional Psychology in Piscataway, New Jersey.

STEVEN GUTSTEIN is a psychologist, autism expert, and director of Connections Center for Family and Personal Development in Houston.

EDWARD M. "NED" HALLOWELL, MD, is a psychiatrist and the founder of the Hallowell Center for Cognitive and Emotional Health in Sudbury, Massachusetts. He is the author of twelve books, including *Driven to Distraction*.

SIDNEY HARMAN is the executive chairman and founder of Harman International Industries in Washington, D.C.

RONALD HEIFETZ is a cofounder of the Center for Public Leadership at Harvard University's John F. Kennedy School of Government in Cambridge, Massachusetts, and a partner at Cambridge Leadership Associates, a consultancy in Cambridge.

ANDREA JUNG is the chair and CEO of Avon Products, which is based in New York.

MANFRED F. R. KETS DE VRIES is the Raoul de Vitry d'Avaucourt Chaired Professor of Leadership Development at Insead in France and Singapore and the director of Insead's Global Leadership Centre. He is also a practicing psychoanalyst who has authored or edited more than twenty books on the psychology of leaders and organizations, including *Life and Death in the Executive Fast Lane* and *The Leadership Mystique*.

JANJA LALICH is an assistant professor of sociology at California State University, Chico, and an expert on cults.

JIM LOEHR, a performance psychologist, is cofounder and CEO of LGE Performance Systems in Orlando, Florida, a consulting firm that applies training principles developed in sports to business executives. He is author of *The Power of Full Engagement* with Tony Schwartz.

JOHN D. MAYER is a professor of psychology at the University of New Hampshire. He and Yale psychology professor Peter Salovey are credited with first defining the concept of emotional intelligence in the early 1990s.

GARDINER MORSE is a senior editor at *Harvard Business Review*.

TONY SCHWARTZ is executive vice president of LGE Performance Systems in Orlando, Florida, a consulting firm that applies training principles developed in sports to business executives. He is author of *What Really Matters: Searching for*

Wisdom in America, Work in Progress with Michael Eisner, and *The Power of Full Engagement* with Jim Loehr.

LINDA STONE is the former vice president of corporate and industry initiatives at Microsoft in Redmond, Washington.

HIROTAKA TAKEUCHI is the dean of Hitotsubashi University's Graduate School of International Corporate Strategy in Tokyo.

MICHAEL TILSON THOMAS is the music director of the San Francisco Symphony.

Index

173